Out at the Library

CELEBRATING THE JAMES C. HORMEL GAY & LESBIAN CENTER

SAN FRANCISCO PUBLIC LIBRARY

This book is published by the San Francisco Public Library in conjunction with the exhibition *Out at the Library: Celebrating the James C. Hormel Gay and Lesbian Center* on view at the San Francisco Main Library and the Eureka Valley/Harvey Milk Memorial Branch Library from June 18–October 16, 2005. The exhibition was organized by the San Francisco Public Library. Sales of this publication benefit the Hormel Center.

The *Out at the Library* catalogue has been made possible by the Dorian Fund, a charitable trust established by Joseph Gianelli and William Wegele to benefit the gay and lesbian community.

Printed by PrintResults, Inc., Portland, OR
First edition

Catalogue editor and designer: Stephanie Snyder
Essays: Judy Grahn and Jim Van Buskirk
Roundtable discussion: Barbara Levine
Texts: Jason Baxter, Everett Erlandson, Léonie Guyer, James C. Hormel, Catherine M. King, Barbara Levine, Stephanie Snyder, Jim Van Buskirk, and Tim Wilson

 For information see page 138.

ISBN 0-9764293-1-4
Library of Congress Control Number: 2005900959

ABOVE:
Hormel Center archives

COVER AND TITLE PAGE:
Maker unknown
Boots worn by Dr. Mary Walker, c.1863
Leather, wood
BARBARA GRIER AND DONNA MCBRIDE/NAIAD PRESS COLLECTION

Contents

EDITED BY STEPHANIE SNYDER

View of Hormel Center

A generation ago, men and women in America were just beginning to realize full political and social expression around issues of sexual orientation and identity. Then, with terrible swiftness, the AIDS pandemic swept in. Many of our most talented and dynamic leaders were taken by the disease. Many others became caregivers. In the immediate backlash we all were harshly reminded that life is precious, and that our movement toward full equality is dependent upon our ability to educate and assist others to overcome ignorance and bigotry.

Foreword

James C. Hormel

During the subsequent campaign for the new San Francisco Main Library, Steven Coulter, then president of the Library Commission, met with a small group to discuss a remarkable idea, namely, to create an affinity group for the library to fund an archival center for materials relating to lesbian, gay, bisexual, and transgender history and culture and documenting the lives of people in our community. Those of us in attendance offered our enthusiastic support, and the concept of an LGBT center at a major public library inspired literally thousands of individuals to develop the project to completion, through years of planning, organizing, and funding.

Nearly ten years later, the Hormel Center has become a primary source of information for all who seek better understanding of the LGBT constituency. Furthermore, it is a sanctuary, inspiring all of us to recognize and claim our history with pride and purpose. Now, every person who reads under the center's mural, conducts research in the archives, attends a program or exhibition, or uses its Web site is part of the present and the future of the center. *Out at the Library*—both the exhibition and this book—displays the riches of the Hormel Center, revealing its extraordinary breadth.

Harvey Milk, in a moving 1977 speech announcing his candidacy for San Francisco Supervisor, said, "I've been running for so many things for so long in this city that I wear a pair of sweats to work ... after all, you can never tell when another opportunity will present itself." Milk's hand-edited speech—part of the center's archives—reminds us that around every corner exists an opportunity for growth. May we recognize these opportunities, and use them to grow.

Douglas Menuez
James C. Hormel
Color photograph

TOP TO BOTTOM:
Study of the Hormel Center mural by Mark Evans and Charley Brown

Hormel Center interior

Introduction

Catherine M. King
Jim Van Buskirk

The book that you are holding marks a milestone: nearly a decade ago, the San Francisco Public Library opened its beautiful new main library at Civic Center. When it was unveiled in April of 1996, among the library's achievements was the James C. Hormel Gay and Lesbian Center. This research center—named for Ambassador James C. Hormel, the renowned philanthropist and community leader—is devoted to collecting, preserving, and providing access to lesbian, gay, bisexual, and transgender history and culture.

The Hormel Center is located in a circular room on the third floor of the main library. It is a ceremonial space, graced with a circular ceiling mural that celebrates LGBT history. The handsome room houses a small selection of published books and magazines, representing a gateway to the wealth of LGBT material physically housed throughout the library. For example, magazines and newspapers are housed on the fifth floor in the Magazines and Newspapers Center, and archival collections (personal papers, organizational records, and photographic portfolios) are accessible in the San Francisco History Center on the sixth floor. Since its opening, the center's collections have continued to grow and develop, their use increasing annually. The schedule of regularly rotating exhibitions and topical public programs attracts widely diverse attendees.

Out at the Library: Celebrating the James C. Hormel Gay and Lesbian Center commemorates the creation and development of this pioneering project, believed to be the first repository of its kind in a public library. This book—and the exhibition it accompanies—highlights the center's history, showcases some of its treasures, and rearticulates its mission. Simultaneously chronicling and celebrating this significant achievement allows the center's archives and programs to illuminate our path into the future.

Acknowledgements

Out at the Library has been a truly collaborative project and was created by the participation, support, and vision of many people. We gratefully acknowledge Barbara Levine who, nearly ten years after curating the Hormel Center's inaugural exhibition *Into the Light*, curated *Out at the Library* and assembled a visionary team to realize the library's goals for this ambitious project. The exhibition team inspired us to envision and interpret our collections in new and inspired ways. The talented group of collaborators brought to this project has exhibited a dedication to the material that has been more than we could have imagined. Stephanie Snyder, catalogue editor and designer, realized the vision of this beautiful publication in dialogue with the exhibition. Léonie Guyer assiduously researched the archives and collaborated on the development of the publication and exhibition. Wendy Miller, permissions manager, expertly secured the book's copyright permissions and contributed to organizing the catalogue's credits and artists' attributions. Allison Dubinsky contributed her talents to copy-editing and proof reading of the catalogue. Dana Davis completed beautiful catalogue photography, and Ira Kleinberg contributed the index. Ron Laster and Rick England brought their expertise and creativity to printing the catalogue. Stephen Jaycox did a masterful job designing the exhibition and interpreting the content in all three San Francisco sites. Cara Storm innovatively marketed the exhibition and David Perry expertly publicized the exhibition to enthusiastic local and national audiences.

Many individuals at the San Francisco Public Library were essential to making *Out at the Library* a reality. We offer sincere thanks to Susan Hildreth, former City Librarian (now California State Librarian) and Paul Underwood, Deputy City Librarian, for their early and unwavering support and to Marcia Schneider, Chief of Communications, Collections and Adult Services, who stood beside us every step of the way. We are also grateful to Chief of the Main Kathy Lawhun and Main Manager of the Third Floor Dennis Maness. We acknowledge the contributions of the many library staff members and community volunteers who over the years helped make LGBT materials available to the public. In particular, City Archivist Susan Goldstein and the staff of the San Francisco History Center deserve special thanks for providing access to materials and assisting with research. We appreciate Hormel Center Processing Archivist Tim Wilson's deep knowledge of the collection and Archivist Jason Baxter's expertise with the Cockettes and Harry Hay collections. We also thank Pat Akre, curator of the San Francisco Historical Photograph Collection, and Andrea Grimes, Book Arts & Special Collections Center Librarian.

We offer thanks to the library's talented exhibitions and programming staff for their expertise and professionalism on all of our projects. This special celebration would not have been possible without the individual and collective contributions of Programs Curator Joan Jasper, Exhibitions Curator Everett Erlandson, and museum preparators Ann Carroll and Maureen Russell. We thank Public Relations Officer Gabrielle Jones, graphic artist Barbara McMahan, and Almer Castillo in Public Affairs for outreach on this project. We thank the media services staff David Schwabe, Eric Monteiro, and Brad Orgeron for their assistance with public programs and to the web team members Joan Lefkowitz, Mike Levy, and Adam Markosian for creating the online exhibition. Thanks also to Karen Sundheim and the staff of the Eureka Valley/Harvey Milk Memorial Branch Library for their ongoing collaboration with the Hormel Center and their participation as an exhibition venue for *Out at the Library*.

Out at the Library would not have been possible without the support and partnership of Friends of the San Francisco Public Library. We thank the Hormel Endowment Committee, a committee of Friends of the Library, for enthusiastically endorsing the project. We thank present and past staff members of Friends of the Library including Kathy Bella, Donna Bero, Colman Conroy, Bobcar Daffeh, Deborah Doyle, Martín Gomez, Catherine Maness, Amy Sollins, Alan Spooner, Byron Spooner, Rand Salwasser, and Clarence Wong as well as fundraising consultants Lisa Hoffman and Brenda Laribee.

This endeavor would not have been realized without the devoted *Out at the Library* Leadership Committee who championed the project and raised the funds needed. Many thanks to cochairs Charles Q. Forester and Jan Zivic, and committee members Jeff Anderson, Alvin H. Baum Jr., Matt Bissinger, Michael Bowen, Steven A. Coulter, Gary Gielow, Jewelle L. Gomez, Bob Hill, Jeff Lewy, Penney Magrane, and Bob Sass.

We are grateful to Ambassador James C. Hormel for generously challenging others to join him in supporting the center's work and we would like to thank all those who made a financial commitment to this project. For sponsoring the *Out at the Library* catalogue we give special thanks to the Dorian Fund, a charitable trust established by Joseph Gianelli and William Wegele to benefit the gay and lesbian community. For their early support of this celebration we thank institutional funders that include the Friends of the San Francisco Public Library, the Gill Foundation, the Evelyn and Walter Haas Jr. Fund, the Walter and Elise Haas Fund, the van Löben Sels/Rembe Rock Foundation, and the Wells Fargo Foundation.

In undertaking this project, we want to acknowledge that it would not have been possible were it not for those who lived their lives courageously, for those who had the foresight to realize that history was being created and for those who preserved and donated documents to be used by future generations.

It has been an honor to work on this project.

Catherine M. King
Out at the Library Project
Director and Chief Curator
San Francisco Public Library

Jim Van Buskirk
Head of the James C. Hormel
Gay and Lesbian Center
San Francisco Public Library

We all have the right to learn about ourselves, yet for lesbian, gay, bisexual, and transgender people, the right to learn about ourselves through texts was withheld for many years until a concerted movement bloomed in the 1970s. A cultural force with its own publications, presses, activists, and politicians opened the door and aroused the incipient urge for change. This awakening resulted in a mass movement of people who have since come to challenge every aspect of gender—socially, politically, spiritually, culturally, and physically.

I came of age in the midst of this repression and subsequent revolution. In *Another Mother Tongue*, I described my banishment in 1961, as a young woman, from my culture's texts: "When I was twenty-one, I went to a library in Washington, D.C., to read about homosexuals and lesbians: to investigate, explore, compare opinions, learn who I might be, what others thought of me, and who my peers were and had been. The books on such a subject, I was told by indignant, terrified librarians unable to say aloud the word *homosexual*, were locked away. They showed me a wire cage where the 'special' books were kept in a jail for books. Only professors, doctors, psychiatrists, and lawyers for the criminally insane could see them, check them out, hold them in their hands." [1]

Tracking Past & Present

Judy Grahn

I couldn't have known at that time that the country was at the tail end of a social cycle as regular as breathing—and that our world was about to open again. I just knew the outrage, roused to a white-hot anger, because we could not read about ourselves, could not learn about, or from, people like ourselves. And so like others of my generation, and those before, and after, I determined to make changes so that we *could* find ourselves—resolute to leave plenty of tracks for others to follow.

A bisexual poet wrote, "tracks here and there/are signs," meaning that impressions left by the lives, knowledge, and spirit of a people, even an oppressed people, continue despite anything: leaving clues, artifacts, and tracks, allowing collective purpose to be found, reassembled, and moved forward with ever-renewed energy. [2] The James C. Hormel Gay and Lesbian Center archives is a rich treasury of exactly such tracks unfurling from simple-seeming objects: personal artifacts, photographs and letters, T-shirts, matchbook covers, and, of all things, Civil War boots. The archives' humble objects are metaphors for larger aspects of LGBT experience.

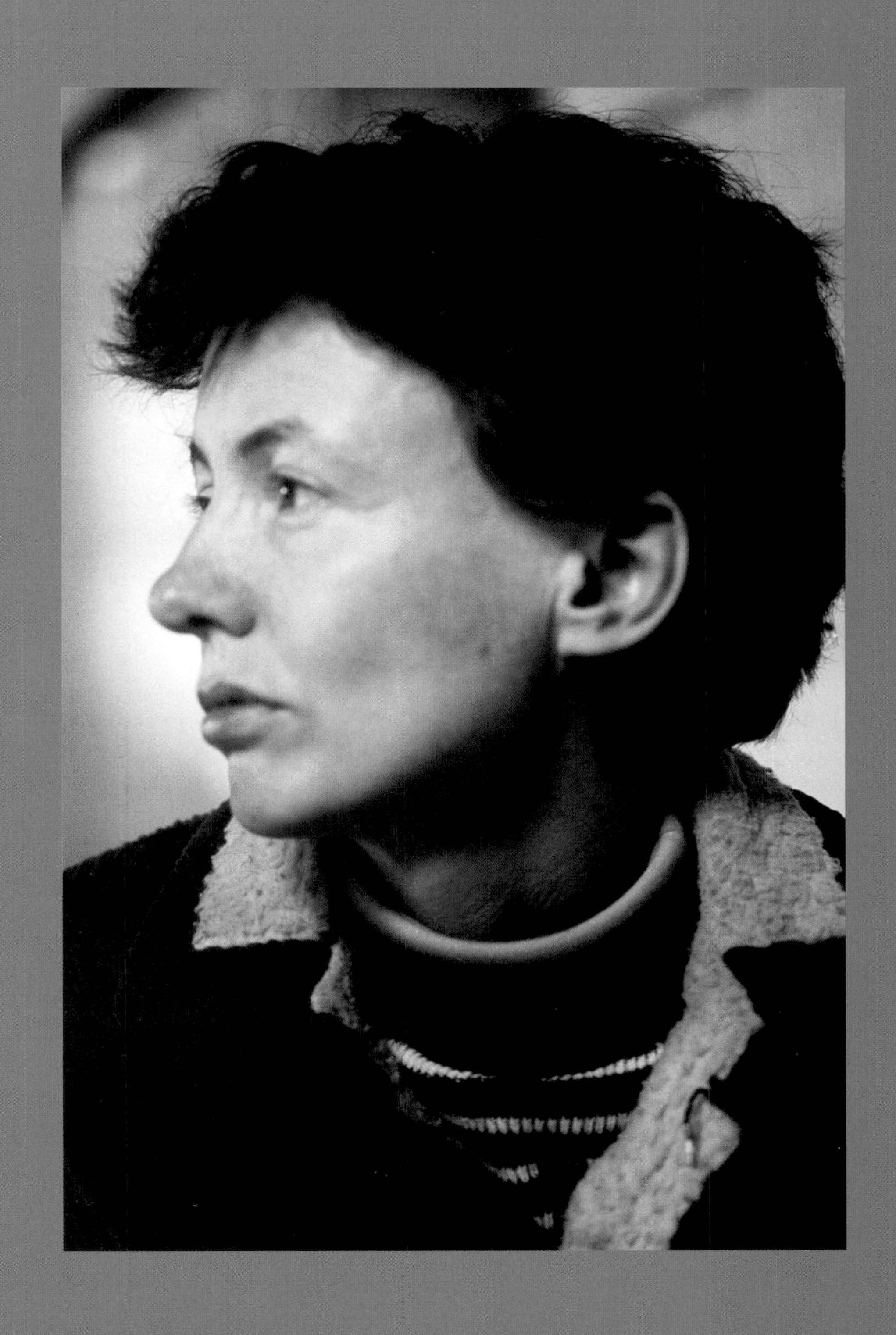

Lynda Koolish
Judy Grahn, c.1972
Gelatin silver print
LYNDA KOOLISH
PHOTOGRAPHS COLLECTION

Harry Hay came to meet me while I was reading from *Another Mother Tongue* on one of my many trips to Los Angeles. More than twenty years before, in 1964, D.C., I had belonged to a cell of the Mattachine Society in Washington, where I was a very young worker bee and had never heard of him. I did not know that he had founded the organization, and later was excluded from it because of his radicalism and cultural perspective. Hay defined gay people as a special group with a great deal to teach heterosexuals.

Now in the mid-1980s, here he sat in the front row, a fascinating, long-legged, bony-kneed, rangy man with white hair, a big fun-looking smile, and quite striking socks. He came up to me afterwards and asked: "Do you know who I am?" When I admitted that I did not, Hay told me his name and almost immediately showed me his socks. They were colorful plaid knee socks, worn with shorts, with something odd about them. Peering down I realized that they came from slightly different pairs. "I wore these for you," Harry said, "to show you how we signaled each other during the thirties. We wore beautiful knee-high socks that didn't match. That was our code. I knew you would be appreciative." He was referring to the signal systems that gay people use. Signs include: little finger rings, the color purple, and subtle linguistic clues like an emphasis on the word "friend." And—I now learned—mismatched, and gorgeously showy, socks that displayed a very particular kind of idiosyncrasy.

These were tracks: the language of clothing, gesture, and innuendo. The costumes denoting difference, the T-shirts declaiming positions: "How dare you assume I am heterosexual?" or "This kind deed is compliments of a bull dyke," or "No, I am not a boy or a girl, are you?" Tracks tell us more than the fact that someone was there before. They tell us that *we* are on a path, a purposeful path, that we are not just wandering around. I believe that LGBT people have trod such paths throughout history, whether secretly, with coded signals, or publicly, as in the current mass movement containing high-profile celebrities and politicians. The cover of this book shows a humble pair of boots that blazed a trail we are still walking.

Surgeon Mary Walker was a small, slender, bright-eyed, courageous, intelligent and caring woman, who wanted to be a fully functioning doctor in the middle of her country's Civil War. She belonged to the gender that had been shut out of almost all professions for generations; she was living in an era decades away from accepting women as doctors. Mary couldn't wait until society changed, so she did the sensible thing: she blurred her gender. Wearing men's clothing, Mary declared herself the equal of a man. She pushed this confiscated privilege to the limit, imitating the dress of a professional man in black top hat and split tail coat, claiming full gentleman's status for herself. By so boldly transvestizing, she opened paths women would continue to follow into the twentieth century, flowing into the occupations of both the military and the medical professions. Her boots, so tiny by our standards, left deep, firm footprints.

From my perspective, human evolution creates tracks that are like strands, especially gendered strands. To work together, these strands need to be braided. In a bipolar two-gendered system, males and females evolve separately, excluding each other from their everyday behaviors and practices. Eventually, intolerable imbalances make them virtually two different peoples, except for the actions of the transgendered—the weavers who catch the extremes of the diverting strands and pull them into alignment, braiding gendered roles in what I call "crossover moves." In these moves, or movements in the larger sense, specialized skills, occupations, subtleties of emotional expression, economic and political status, varieties of personal and social power, and so on, are transferred from one gender to the other. This keeps human achievement spinning.

This same cross-gendered braiding existed in indigenous cultures, often in socially designated "offices" or accepted functions, including shamans, priests, advisors to chiefs, warrior women, visionaries, and handlers of the dead. "Ceremonial offices," (to borrow a

Photographer unknown
Photograph from
Sylvester's wedding
Golden Gate Park
San Francisco, CA, 1972
Pictured: Billy Orchid, Pristine Condition, Sweet Pam, Scrumbly
KREEMAH RITZ PAPERS

term contributed to LGBT discourse by Paula Gunn Allen from Native American usage) stretch as far back in time as early writing. A Mesopotamian text dated 2300 B.C.E. records a "head overturning" rite exalting the major deity Inanna. Mesopotamian temple rituals of weeping and singing were deemed the province of persons Inanna herself had ritually created as cross-gendered. In medieval India, a special caste of transgendered she-men—the *hijra*—guarded and otherwise served in the all-women's harems; and in China eunuchs became a powerful political force into the ninth century. These are just a few of the braided tracks that have been left for us.

And cross-gendered braiding is just as powerful in contemporary culture. For example, in the 1970s in Atlanta, writer Steve Abbott wore a gown with a full beard to a wedding; and Harry Hay wore a string of pearls with his men's clothing before 1950, just as I and women like me wore a ducktail haircut and men's loafers in the rigidly sex-roled atmosphere of Washington, D.C. in 1961—these high risk gestures served as magnets for intensely quizzical attention (including invitations to public beatings), and all, in their time and place, left tracks that cracked open gender polarities.

Harvey Milk's handwritten notes chronicle his months in office as the first out gay man to hold an elected position in San Francisco. Though Harvey Milk and Harry Hay might have been on opposite sides of the cultural/political divide, they both championed the

SUPERVISOR HARVEY MILK
CITY HALL, SAN FRANCISCO

1.

ON ONE HAND THERE IS FREEDOM OF SPEECH, HUMAN RIGHTS, AND THE RIGHT TO PRIVACY....ON THE OTHER HAND THERE IS PROPOSITION 6 which is a MISGUIDED, CONFUSED, DANGEROUS, DECEITFULL, FRIGHTENING, AND UN-AMERICAN ATTACH ON BASIC HUMAN RIGHTS..THE SAME KIND THAT SPAWNED WITCHHUNTS, NAZISM, MCCARTHYISM.....AND AS EDUCATOR AFTER EDUCATOR, LEGISLATOR AFTER LEGISLATOR, RELIGIOUS LEADER AFTER REGLISOUS LEADER HAS STATED: IT IS COMPLELTLEY UNNECCESSARY BECAUSE THERE ARE ALREADY LAWS AND ENFORCEABLE LAWS ON THE BOOKS TO PROTECT OUR CHILDREN.

IT COMES FROM THE SAME TACTICS THAT NIXON USED TO REACH THE U.S. SENATE... A SELF SERVING POLITICIAN DREAMING UP A "MORAL" CRUSADE TO RIDE TO POWER... NIXON CHASES NON EXISTING COMMUNISTS OUT FROM UNDER OUR BEDS AND ONLY ALL TOO LATE WE FOUND OUT ABOUT HIS OWN PERSONAL MORALITY...NOW WE HAVE A PERSON WHO IS FULL OF CONTRIDICTION AFTER CONTRIDICTION TRYING TO USE THE GAY COMMUNITY AS SCAPEGOATS TO SATISFY HIS MORAL CRUSDAE IN AN ATTEMPT TO RUN FOR HIGHER OFFICE

SUPERVISOR HARVEY MILK
CITY HALL, SAN FRANCISCO

2

IF THIS IS ALLOWED TO PASS IT COULD BECOME PAERT OF AN EPIDEMIC WHICH WILL SPREAD _ AS IT DID IN NAZI GERMANY _ TO OTHER INDIVIDUALS WHO ARE MINORITIES BY VIRTURE OF THEIR RACE, RELIGION, SEX, POLITICAL BELIEVES, OR NATIONAL ORIGIN.

AND JOHN BRIGGS IN HIS DESPIRICATION KEEPS CHANGING HIS TUNE FROM DAY TO DAY AS EACH AND E ERY ONE OF HIS ARGUEMNTS FALLS APART AND MYTH AFTER MYTHE IS SHATTERED BY FACTS SO THAT NOW HE IS NO LONGER TAKING ISSUES AN FACTS BUT PLAYING UPON WORDS AND WORDS ONLY TO THE POINT WHERE HE HAS R EACHED THE LEVEL OF MCCARTHISM HIMSELF TOSSING OUT LIES, INNUEDNOES ANDBEING HYPOCTITCAL HIMSELF TRYING TO PLAY UPON PEOPLES FEARS BASED UPON MYTHS...JOHN BRIGGS KNOWS HE IS DOING THIS ..HE KNOWS THAT HE IS PLAYING UPON FEARS BASED UPON MYTHS AND NOT FACTS AND THUS IS NOT ONLY OUT AND OUT LYING BUT BY USING HIS MORAL CRUSDAE TO DO SO HE HAS BECOME

Harvey Milk
Hand-edited speech on Briggs debate regarding Proposition 6
c.1978
HARVEY MILK ARCHIVES–SCOTT SMITH COLLECTION

lives of ordinary working people. Harvey said of the gay movement developing in San Francisco during the 1970s, "we must give people the chance to judge us by our leaders and legislators. A gay person in office can set a tone, can command respect not only from the larger community, but from the young people in our own community who need both examples and hope." [3] Once elected to the Board of Supervisors in 1977, Milk lived his populist philosophy, working on behalf of all minorities for a participatory democracy with equitable opportunities. Following the light sentence that Milk's assassin received, riots in San Francisco showed the determination as well as the strength and unity of a movement that would never be content until all its members received full rights of citizenship and participation in democratic processes, including, most recently, rights of marriage and parenting.

Many years ago I started my own journey along a line of continuing research, from a list of twelve words that I had been called in my life, including: *gay, butch, faggot*. Words, even when intended to insult and intimidate, become tracks. Someone else might start a research project with a matchbook from a particular bar frequented, say, by Sammy Steward, who left his mark in several places. As a young man he became friends with Gertrude Stein and Alice B. Toklas, writing about them later in his life. He became a professor at Loyola University, then left that life and changed his name to Phil Sparrow in order to plunge into an underworld of tattoo artists, using his skill on the backs and forearms of Hell's Angels, among other skin canvases. Sammy influenced some of the best tattoo artists of today's high art form, while continuing to write gay erotica under the pen name of Phil Andros. Other major literary figures like Allen Ginsberg, Walt Whitman, Audre Lorde, and Alice Walker, are infinitely important to all of society; they are leaders. To recognize them as LGBT individuals and artists is to recognize their contribution to the world at large. Once people can see and place themselves in the past, the future opens out before them. We begin to understand *ourselves* as signs, moving on purposeful paths.

In the 1970s, African American lesbian poet and activist Pat Parker told me how she thought history should be written. In Parker's view, every group, representing every facet of society, should write a chapter set in the same era so that all points of view would be present. Surely, Parker felt, a basic human right is to be *represented* historically. From there extends the right to know what is being written and recorded about oneself, and one's culture, and the right to interpret and contribute to one's history, through artifacts, films, books, and articles. Thanks to collections like the James C. Hormel Gay and Lesbian Center archives, our tracks, signs, thoughts, accomplishments, and artifacts, will not be lost. In such critical sanctuaries, we can find and define ourselves, over and over.

1 Grahn, Judy. *Another Mother Tongue: Gay Words, Gay Worlds*. Boston: Beacon Press, 1984. Preface xi.

2 Gunn Allen, Paula. "Creation Story," in *Shadow Country*. University of California, 1982. pp. 3-4.

3 Quoted in Shilts, Randy. *The Mayor of Castro Street: The Life and Times of Harvey Milk*. New York: St. Martin's Press, 1982. p. 362.

Hormel Center interior

From the Beginning

The James C. Hormel Gay and Lesbian Center

A Roundtable Discussion with Hormel Center Founders

Having curated the Hormel Center's inaugural exhibition *Into the Light: The Making of the Mural*, it is especially meaningful for me to return to the Library as curator of *Out at the Library*, celebrating the first ten years of the Hormel Center. It was an honor then to be involved with the opening of the first gay and lesbian center in a San Francisco civic building and it is an honor now to reflect on the important community resource that the James C. Hormel Gay and Lesbian Center has become.

On the occasion of *Out at the Library: Celebrating the James C. Hormel Gay and Lesbian Center*, the library thought that it would be wonderful to gather the center's founders for a conversation about the history and future of the Hormel Center. The following conversation took place on November 16, 2004, at the San Francisco Main Library. Gathered were: Steven A. Coulter, Charles Q. Forester, Kathy Page, Jim Van Buskirk, and Jan Zivic.
—Barbara Levine

Barbara Levine: It is nearing the ten-year anniversary of the opening of the San Francisco Public Library's James C. Hormel Gay and Lesbian Center. The goal of our discussion today is to hear your reflections on what it was like to create the center, essentially from start to completion. The five of you were there from the very beginning—each representing different aspects of the project—from crafting the vision and fundraising, to ensuring that the center would be ready for the opening of the new library. So much has happened in the lesbian, gay, bisexual, and transgender communities in the last ten years, and the struggle for equal rights continues. This is also an opportunity for us to look forward together, and to discuss the future of the center. To get started, when did each of you become involved with the Hormel Center project? What was your role then, and what are you doing now?

Steve Coulter: At the time I was first involved with the Hormel Center, I wore two hats: Art Agnos [former mayor of San Francisco] appointed me president of the Library Commission in 1988, and I was also vice president of external affairs for Pacific Bell. It was my PacBell role that allowed me to get so heavily involved with the San Francisco Public Library. Today, I am still a library commissioner. I am basically retired, although I do a lot of volunteer work and some consulting.

Kathy Page: I was the chief of facilities development for the library. I was on the library staff from 1989 to 1997, and I got involved in the project when I started working at the library in 1989. In January of 1990, when there was a delegation that went to visit exemplary libraries in Europe, I got an opportunity to talk to Steve Coulter, and that's when it began. I was involved from the moment that he told me of his idea. I am now a library planning consultant, principal of Kathryn Page Associates.

Jim Van Buskirk: I was a staff member at the library when the idea for the Hormel Center was first proposed. I was also involved in many of the early acquisitions for the archives. I was named the center's first program manager—a position that I still hold.

Jan Zivic: I was an executive search consultant and director of Spencer Stuart Consulting in 1994 when Sherry Thomas, from the Library Foundation, called me to ask if I might be interested in joining the fundraising committee for the project. I am now retired and am doing full-time fundraising and am serving as the cochair of the *Out at the Library* Leadership Committee.

Chuck Forester: My involvement began at a meeting at Steve Coulter's house, I believe in 1991, to talk about the idea of putting together a gay and lesbian center in the library. Steve had a commitment from Mayor Agnos to develop such a center, and he wondered if we thought it was possible to raise money to facilitate it. I was the chair of the board of the Human Rights Campaign and active in fundraising and nonprofit work in the community. I became the chairman of the Founders Committee for the Hormel Center, and currently I am the cochair of the *Out at the Library* Leadership Committee.

Daniel Nicoletta
Harvey clowning around in his
Castro Street camera store
February, 1977
Gelatin silver print
DANIEL NICOLETTA
PHOTOGRAPHS COLLECTION

Barbara Levine: So from 1988 onward, almost ten years before the Hormel Center opened, there was a lot going on behind the scenes in terms of crafting a vision, strategizing a plan, and assembling a group of people to manifest both. I know, Steve, that you were very influenced by the Schomburg Center for Research in Black Culture at the New York Public Library. What were the goals and first visions for the Hormel Center?

Steve Coulter: In 1988, Art Agnos, the mayor of San Francisco—a very liberal, populist individual—wanted the library and all city institutions to open their arms, find new constituencies, and connect with underserved populations. It was a political goal of his, and those he appointed, like me, carried these goals as marching orders walking in. The Library Commission at the time, made up of like-minded people, saw the building of a new main library as an opportunity to open up the institution differently than it had been before.

Hormel Center archives

As part of my role as president of the commission, I visited libraries around the country when I traveled for business as an executive at Pacific Bell, and I tried to see what people were doing. I was, indeed, taken by the New York Public Library, among others. The Schomburg Center for Research in Black Culture is an amazing institution focused on the black community—a separate institution, if you will, but within the public library of New York. I was taken with their programs and had a number of meetings with people there.

In San Francisco, we divided up different library branches for the commissioners to become familiar with. Eureka Valley/Harvey Milk Memorial Branch was the one that logically fell to me since it was my neighborhood branch. They had made an effort to develop a gay and lesbian collection there—mostly old newspapers and other kinds of materials. They also had an advisory committee, and I attended one of their meetings and laid out a kind of "gay Schomburg" idea with them. Some people liked the idea, some people didn't. Sherry Thomas was a member of that committee and she was the publisher of the *Spinster's Ink*. Jim Van Buskirk was a member of that committee. Roberto Esteves, as a senior library official, came with me to the meeting and participated in early discussions. Kathy Page was very supportive of the concept early on. Ken Dowlin, the city librarian, was supportive. The mayor loved it, to say the least, and his whole senior staff loved it. Agnos is an important figure. He heard our ideas and said, "This is exactly the kind of thing I want to see. My commissioner is doing it and my commission is doing it."

We started talking to people like Chuck here, and others, to develop interest. Could we raise the money? What would this center be like? The basic goal was that we needed a gay equivalent of the Schomburg Center. This idea floated around for probably a couple of years before we were ready to move ahead. The Library Commission included in its five-year plan the concept of developing special collections around the main collections within the library. So the gay and lesbian center per se wasn't our first priority, but it was on our list of goals to accomplish over the next six years.

Barbara Levine: It's wonderful to hear you describe the civic foundations and community groundwork from which the center emerged. Do you remember the emotions that you had at the time and what inspired you to make a commitment to the project?

Chuck Forester: I had been working for a number of years with Martin Paley, who was originally the head of the San Francisco Foundation and then became the executive director of the Library Foundation. During that time we had been focusing on helping various communities talk to each other. With all the diversity in town there were still divisions, and growing divisions, between the black, gay and lesbian, Italian, and Chinese communities, to name a few. We had formed a group called San Franciscans Seeking Consensus that brought together leaders from all of these groups.

When Martin became active in the library campaign, it was very natural to include the vision of bringing the communities of San Francisco together on a project. We talked out all kinds of things that we agreed on, but when it came time to actually doing something, the committee never really got going. The library provided the perfect opportunity for all the communities of San Francisco to really work together. So the idea for the gay center really encouraged thinking about similar initiatives for the Chinese community, the Latino community, and other communities in town.

I had also been doing a lot of fundraising on the political side, so this seemed like a perfect match for me. It was something that was very easy to believe in at a time when the gay community was in the middle of the AIDS epidemic—we were not certain whether any of us were going to be around in the future. The idea of an archives in which we preserved who we were gave us a sense of the future that was very hard to come by then. Also, having a place where we would be recognized publicly as living entities—my name next to my partner's name, Jan's name next to her partner's name—was very important. At that time, gay names were in public on the AIDS quilt—they were memorialized *after death*. That was the kind of recognition we were getting in those days.

Barbara Levine: That's an important point you make about being public and visible. What kind of impact did that have on you personally and professionally?

Jan Zivic: That's actually why I thought about *not* joining. When Sherry Thomas called to ask me to join the committee, I was not out as a lesbian in terms of my professional life, and I worked in a very straight, male-dominated world. So I said I wouldn't join. But I came to a meeting and was so impressed by the people that were there that I said, "OK, I'm in—and I'm out!" It was that simple. I knew it was going to be a public effort that was going to succeed. And although I came in after the vision and the ball got rolling, I was very emotional about the fact that, as Chuck just mentioned, it was the first time that a city municipality was saying, "We are going to work together with the gay community and be public about this and we are going to be a model for the rest of the country."

Barbara Levine: Kathy, what was it like for you to be on the library staff at that time?

Kathy Page: Well, being a librarian, it was really moving being involved. I've been a librarian since the early seventies, and it was always a fight to acquire and keep gay and lesbian materials. Sexual preference was always marginalized and not really spoken of, although quite a few gays and lesbians worked at libraries. So this was an opportunity to do something remarkably different and honor our community.

Chuck Forester: Here's an interesting anecdote about the fundraising. After a meeting at Steve's house, I remember sitting at Zuni Café and, quite literally on the back of a napkin, figuring out how much money we needed to raise. Those figures were presented back to the Library Foundation. Dr. Arthur Coleman, a leading civil rights advocate and one of the earliest leaders in the African American community here, was on the foundation board, and he heard about our goal of $1.6 million. The African American community had done some sort of assessment of how much money they could raise, based on political campaigns, and they had been advised that they might be able to raise $25,000. When Arthur Coleman heard that we were going to raise $1.6 million he said, "We're going raise at least $500,000," and they did—they raised $600,000. Not only were we working for our community, we were providing a stimulus for other communities in San Francisco and across the bay.

Steve Coulter: The Library Foundation thought the idea of a gay and lesbian center was terrific, but they were afraid of fundraising for a niche project when they were trying to raise money for the good of the whole. Martin Paley really loved the project and wanted to find a way to raise money for both. As Chuck said, we came up with a formula that other affinity groups used after us. We asked ourselves, "How much money do you need for the room itself?" Which was $250,000, and then we thought, "OK, we will raise more money for the library as a whole because gay and lesbian books, videotapes, microfilm, magazines, and children's books will be placed throughout the institution so we need to put more money in for these." So we set a million-dollar goal. We only needed $250,000 for the room, but we set a million-dollar goal. Then the discussion emerged that we needed to develop an endowment. So out of the blue, I don't know where it came from, we decided $600,000 would be the endowment we would try to raise to reach a $1.6 million goal. It was very ambitious.

Chuck Forester: At the time, the community had gotten involved in fundraising in a big way in terms of the AIDS epidemic, and we said very clearly that we didn't want a dime of

Daniel Nicoletta
Native American Indian advocate Randy Burns and friend at San Francisco Queer Pride Parade, June 25, 2000
Gelatin silver print
DANIEL NICOLETTA PHOTOGRAPHS COLLECTION

Microfilm storage

HERB CAEN MAGAZINES

AND NEWSPAPERS CENTER

anyone's money that would otherwise go to an AIDS organization. And that was never an issue. Nobody stopped giving to an AIDS organization, but almost everybody gave to this. And I think, if I remember correctly, that the second largest group of donors to this library outside of Northern California came from Washington, D.C.

Barbara Levine: Not only was your blueprint a template for other groups, it worked toward the library's mission of benefiting underserved communities. People felt very excited about doing something for the first time and being public and resourceful for a project that looked to the future. As you prepared to open the center, what were some particularly memorable thoughts or events?

Kathy Page: One of my favorite memories is the night of the party, right before we opened, remember that? Coming up Grove Street and seeing the Market Street façade flooded with colored lights like the rainbow flag? It was amazing. I have a picture of that hanging in my office.

Jan Zivic: I just got chills hearing you describe it. Really, it was extraordinary.

Steve Coulter: And at the opening there was a ribbon all the way across the rotunda and Jim Hormel cut it to officially open the Hormel Center. I mean, everyone was crying.

Barbara Levine: I was there too. It was extremely moving. I had been in San Francisco about fifteen years and there had been so many tough times—Harvey Milk's assassination and the AIDS epidemic—and I remember, for the first time in a long time, feeling a sense of hopefulness about the future. How was it for you personally, after all those years of making this vision happen, to be standing there at the opening watching everybody experience what you had created?

Chuck Forester: It was very humbling for me, seeing all of us together in a place that was truly ours—not only ours in the moment, but ours throughout time. I felt so humbled and so big—so connected with all of our history, even though a lot of it we don't know yet.

Creating the center, magnificent as it was, caused concern too. The GLBT Historical Society was very concerned that we were creating a collection in a civic space that, over time, might not last. Political winds change, as we saw too poignantly in the last national election, and people were worried that there would someday be a mayor and a board of supervisors that would try to get rid of the center and the collection. So, rightly, the GLBT Historical Society was very concerned that it be protected. I think the library did an outstanding job of negotiating with the GLBT Historical Society to set up a system in which their material could be available at the center but would be protected in case something horrible happened.

Jan Zivic: Wasn't that part of Jim Hormel's vision—that the money be given for the center only if it was guaranteed that, no matter what, the center would continue?

Steve Coulter: We set up an advisory committee that would withhold the money if the center were ever in jeopardy. Chuck, you've talked about this historically. In pre-World War II Europe the first set of books burned in Berlin belonged to Magnus Hirschfeld, a gay collector. Could that ever happen here? We would like to think not, but as you just pointed out, given the recent Republican victory and the fact that gays and lesbians are basically the new Communists, things can change when you least expect them to.

I remember Randy Shilts saying at the 1991 kick-off press conference at the old library, "We're losing far too many people to the AIDS epidemic. It is essential we not lose our history, too." I think Shilts captures, so succinctly, our drive to make sure that the center would never disappear—this project drove people to want to manifest something permanent.

As we began collecting material for the archives, so many people got involved. Marvin Liebman, who wrote *Coming Out Conservative,* came out here for an event for his new book, so we spoke with him and he said, "Of course I want to give you my stuff." And then a box of material arrived about a week later and it is now in the collection, which is great.

We need to remember that we had been denied our history—and here was a mayor and a public institution that was stepping up and saying, "Not only is your history important, but we want to gather it, catalogue it, and we want to create programs with it. We want to celebrate your history." The center's original brochure talked about preserving our history, celebrating our achievements, and strengthening our freedom, and I think all of these are still vital goals ten years after the center was founded.

Barbara Levine: I am amazed by Dr. Mary Walker's boots—the turn-of-the-century, worn leather boots donated by Barbara Grier. For the exhibition team, these boots have become an iconic object for the project. What's so special about them is the way they embody Dr. Walker's steely determination to live life as she saw fit: as a cross-dressing Civil War surgeon. But they also have a delicacy and femininity about them that is charming and vulnerable. They represent the complexity of identity and the grit of hard work.

Lynda Koolish
Joy Harjo, Berkeley, CA
Watershed poetry event, 2002
Gelatin silver print
LYNDA KOOLISH
PHOTOGRAPHS COLLECTION

Kathy Page: What I love most in the collection are the pulp paperbacks. I have my own collection—probably every lesbian in town has her own collection—but these are all in such good condition. Looking at the cover art and reading the outlandish titles is such a pleasure.

Chuck Forester: For me, one eye-opener that the collection has provided is learning about the important role—within the lesbian community—of lesbian publishers such as Naiad Press and other lesbian presses. I don't think this phenomenon was as true for men. Gay men had bars and gyms and other ways of meeting people and trading stories. The importance of the literary world for women is so impressive—how their stories get told and retold and how they talk to each other through books and periodicals as much as through other means.

Barbara Levine: Was the goal of the center from the beginning to have a collection, or did the idea of having a collection evolve as more people got excited about the new center?

Chuck Forester: I think that the library staff made efforts to define and build a collection from the beginning. Sherry Thomas, because she was a publisher herself, knew publishers Barbara Grier and Donna McBride, and she knew the value of having a collection.

Steve Coulter: Of the original fundraising goal of $1.6 million, including the $600,000 in endowment, the purpose of the endowment was precisely to mount exhibitions and to acquire materials for the collection.

Barbara Levine: Was the acquisitions fund earmarked for a specific project or for an extended collecting effort?

Kathy Page: It was for enduring development of an ongoing collection. One of the challenges from the get-go, and not just for the Hormel Center, was that the collections were multidisciplinary by nature and the library had a responsibility to collect for adults, teens, and children, and in all sorts of formats. Could you put everything that could conceivably have gay and lesbian content in one place? And the answer was, no, you can't. Or do you distribute it and link it electronically, bibliographically? We talked endlessly about how to do this. It was always an assumption that we would have materials associated with the center; it was a matter of what the scope and what the profile of those materials would be. In a way, the collection of the Hormel Center radiates throughout the entire building and the entire library system, as does the African American collection, as does the environmental collection.

Chuck Forester: There were a couple of people who said, "We shouldn't have gay material segregated in the library." I think that this came from a kind of fear of being out. And we said, "No—if it is a gay author who wrote a cookbook, it's going to be in the cookbook section. If it's an astronomy book by a queer astronomer, it will be in the astronomy section."

Barbara Levine: I understand that when collecting began in earnest in 1991, the center was looking for gay, lesbian, bisexual, and transgender material. Your emphasis was to be inclusive of these different communities and to acknowledge that the gay and lesbian community had many facets. What were the discussions around the naming of the center? In light of the fact that currently the term "gay and lesbian" has been expanded to include gay, lesbian, bisexual, and transgender, has there been any thought to renaming the center?

Steve Coulter: As the major donor, Jim Hormel was at first reluctant to have the center named for him. There was a lot of discussion and research looking for names that would be appropriate for the center—we looked at Native American languages, you name it—trying to find the perfect thing. We didn't come up with something that we were happy with. Then people basically convinced Jim to use his name.

If you look at the names that this community is called or will be called, it's constantly changing. If you go back seventy years we were all perverts, pansies, what have you. Then you start seeing the terms "homosexual" and "gay" getting picked up, although it took the *New York Times* ten years before it would start using the word *gay*. Then you see the women's community sort of feeling left out, so "gay and lesbian" became the norm. Then the term "queer" becomes the norm. And then you start hearing more about transgender issues, particularly in San Francisco, and bisexual issues. I think "the Gay and Lesbian Center" was appropriate.

The NAACP went through this twenty years ago. The issue was, is "colored people" a good descriptor? What about "black," "Negro," or "African American"? Should they change their name or not? The organization came down with, no, it's historical—we will continue to be the National Association for the Advancement of Colored People. At the same time, though, it's understandable why people want to "see" themselves in a name. But the danger is, if you start changing your name every few years it can get confusing and inconsistent. Most of the country is still probably struggling with the term "gay," much less "gay and lesbian," much less "gay, lesbian, bisexual, and transgender." To those of us in the community it means something. It is very important. This is a complicated question to which there is no simple answer.

Barbara Levine: Jim, as the first and thus far only program manager of the Hormel Center, talk a bit about the audiences that the collection serves and what it is like for you to steward the collection and be looking at the material and interacting with the public at the center.

Jim Van Buskirk: Well, these are issues we wrestled with as we developed the center. Who would be using this material? How are they going to come at it? What are the subject terms we want to apply? We spent a lot of effort dealing with the fact that the Library of Congress subject headings were inadequate for our purposes. So we made a big effort and, at least for the Barbara Grier material, augmented all those titles with additional subject headings. My example was that if someone comes in and wants to find lesbian mysteries set in San Francisco, they need to be able to do it, and before we augmented the subject headings, they couldn't. So we used the Hennepin County subject headings in order to expand our offerings and make the collection more accessible.

In terms of the diversity issues that you mentioned, these have always been at the forefront of the center's goals. As part of my education working with the growing material, I coauthored with Susan Stryker the book *Gay by the Bay*, and that was a crash course in Transgenderism 101. I started meeting bisexuals and understanding how they move through the world and how they see their identity. I have learned so much by working with people, working with materials, and putting people in touch with materials.

Barbara Levine: So here we are, nearly ten years later, and a lot has happened. What are your thoughts about the importance of the center now and your hopes and dreams for the future?

Steve Coulter: The center is an important symbol of the importance of gay and lesbian history and I think it has done well in this regard. Jim Van Buskirk and others have done a terrific job with the exhibitions we've had every year. This exhibition will be the largest we've ever had, and it would be wonderful if it could travel to other institutions. I think traveling this exhibition, particularly in light of the election, is really important. We'll be reaching out to the library world and talking about gay and lesbian, transgender, and bisexual issues from the viewpoint of a public library, and I think we're going to be playing an important role.

Kathy Page: In my work as a library consultant—I work with a lot of municipalities and libraries in planning new facilities—I frequently run into people who want to use the center as a model, and not necessarily regarding gay and lesbian material. Whenever anyone talks about the library, they talk about the center. People know about the Hormel Center.

Jan Zivic: I think, too, that those of us who worked on the center are constantly promoting it; I am a constant ambassador wherever I am in the world. As I meet other gay and lesbian people, they say, "What should we do in San Francisco?" I always bring it up because it is unique. I think people actually do, on their tourist attraction list, include the library and include the center.

the LESBIAN TIDE
JUNE 35¢ 1972
HERE I AM
MOM

patrick
Another traditional family.
GLAAD
Gay and Lesbian Alliance Against Defamation

TOP TO BOTTOM:
The Lesbian Tide
Los Angeles:
The Tide Collective, 1972

Chloe Atkins
GLAAD Billboard ("Another Traditional Family"), 1992
Gelatin silver print
CHLOE ATKINS
PHOTOGRAPHS COLLECTION

Steve Coulter: One of the most amazing documents in the archives is the first comment book that Jim Van Buskirk put out at the center. When people visit the center they could sign up and make comments and some of the comments are really amazing—they bring tears to your eyes. People from around the world say things like: "It's amazing that a city would do this, I am so proud."

Jim Van Buskirk: You can walk into the center and find people sitting, not moving, not speaking, some of them in tears. It may be the first time they have been in a space in a public building devoted to them, about them. They feel safe here. It is indescribable.

Chuck Forester: I think for a lot of people the center is a symbol of hope. Two years ago, maybe three years ago now, the Hormel Center hosted a conference for gay and lesbian Muslims. We had people from all over the world here—people who could be killed at home for being gay. They saw themselves together for the first time in one place and it was this place.

This reminds me of Jim Hormel's confirmation hearings in the U.S. Senate, when he was appointed as the ambassador to Luxembourg. They used the existence of the Hormel Center against him because it contained the *Cunt Coloring Book* and all these "terrible" things. As we go forward we're going to hear more of that right now with this president and this congress. This is a place of hope for the future and we need to keep it that way.

Steve Coulter: Regarding the story of Jim Hormel's hearings—which is part of our archives as well as the Gay and Lesbian Historical Society of Northern California's archives (now the GLBT Historical Society)—Jim Hormel stood firm. He never backed off. He never equivocated. He said, "Yes, I am part of the Gay and Lesbian Center at the library and I am proud of my involvement." Even as the Republicans were bashing him and trying to get him to back off on a whole lot of things in order to move his confirmation ahead, he stuck with it.

I remember that at one of our early donor events, Sir Ian McKellan, the great Shakespearean actor, talked about growing up in England and going to his library and how all he could find out about people like himself were books that talked about perverts. He said that he was very moved to see this sort of thing happening in the United States and in San Francisco and how important it is for young people who are questioning what they are sexually to be able to walk into a public building as beautiful as this one and find, in one of the most beautiful rooms in the library, the gay and lesbian center.

At the entrance to the library on Larkin Street, we have now put up a number of plaques called "the Wall of Library Heroes" and "A Brief History of the Library," and in there we talk a little bit about this center. And in addition to some of the names we mentioned I want to add: Al Baum, Gary Gielow, Jim Haas, Dorwinn Jones, Bob Sass, and Diane Benjamin.
Jim Van Buskirk: The entire library staff was incredible. Everybody went to the limit and

past it. In addition to David McFarland, another person that I would like to mention is Faun McInnis. I reported to her for a while and we would have meeting after meeting about every aspect of the center, and she was right there the whole time.

Jan Zivic: That reminds me also, we talked about what it meant to us, and at least for me, having come out around the whole thing. We would have fundraisers for the library, not just for the Hormel Center, and straight people, gay people, politicians, and celebrities like Carol Burnett—everyone was there. And we were all doing it together. In those rooms there was no distinction about which affinity center—which we were calling the center at that time—you were supporting. We were just all working together for this incredible new main library in San Francisco. It was wonderful.

Steve Coulter: Martin Paley united the city in a great civic campaign as leaders, not as followers. I think of the great African American leader Arthur Coleman talking about how this was the first time that he had been invited to join an important community cause—not as an afterthought, not chasing the caboose after the train had left the station—but as a first class passenger on the journey. I thought Coleman really made a statement about what this was all about.

That said, there were a lot of people, some staff, some from the outside, that really hated the idea of the "ghettoization" of social groups, as some called it, of individually paying attention to homosexuals, blacks, Filipinos, and others. So it was not uncontroversial—the whole approach.

Jan Zivic: I remember the dinner I cochaired with Mark Leno, we had fourteen hundred people there and he announced that this was the most successful fundraising effort we had ever had other than an AIDS or a Barbra Streisand event. The library raised more money than any other event, not just gay and lesbian, that the city had had. We raised over $700,000 that night.

Barbara Levine: Everyone involved was and continues to be very dedicated, passionate, and intelligent about the Hormel Center. The center's upcoming tenth anniversary exhibition and catalogue are so important, because the current generation and future generations not only come to the center to feel safe, they come to experience—firsthand—the history of our culture. Gay and lesbian culture is challenging because often history is being made at the same time that it is being interpreted. It can be difficult to get perspective on events, which is very different from other, older cultures. What do you think is the importance of the Hormel Center now and the importance of the center for young people?

Chuck Forester: Typically, ethnic and religious groups have traditions that are passed down through parents, teachers, and religious leaders. People grow up *with* their culture. They know their cuisine; they know their ethnic history, whatever it is. We don't. We all come from a lot of different places. And we don't think of ourselves as gay until our teens, maybe, sometimes later in life. Our parents don't tell us how to be gay. Our teachers tell us not to be gay. Our religious leaders condemn us for being gay. So a place like this fosters our sense of community. I don't know if kids are going to come and use it, but I think they're going to sit down at their computers and go to the Internet and look up "gay" and this is going to come up.

Jim Van Buskirk: I know that the center acts as a beacon. There may be people who never set foot in this building or never make it to the Web site, but they know that the center is here. I get calls from people all over the country—reference questions—for whom the center is the first place they think of to get information about gay and lesbian history, culture, and experience. I think that's very significant. The Hormel Center is not something that they have in their community physically, but they use it nonetheless.

Steve Coulter: Institutionally we have put in place something that will gather gay and lesbian history and archive it, and periodically celebrate it—but it will remain here and it will grow over time—eventually becoming a Schomburg-like institution, with its own building and a fairly decent-sized staff. I hope that young people will be interested in this.

One thing that's important about a public library doing this is that this material is not at a university where you've got to be a student to have access to the collection. This is open to anyone, and that's part of the excitement. A lot of the donors really liked that idea—having it so that anyone could come in and work with the material.

Jan Zivic: In addition to the Hormel Center, we now have gay and lesbian material all through the library. A young person can walk into the children's center and find *Heather Has Two Mommies* or *Daddie's Roommate*. They find, in a public space, information about their unique kind of family, which up to that point they might have thought was embarrassingly unusual. We have to continue to support that.

Barbara Levine: In doing this project it has been fascinating to navigate the library; I was pleasantly surprised to find that gay, lesbian, bisexual, and transgender materials are not isolated in the Hormel Center. What makes LGBT culture distinct is the network of relationships between people and groups yielding powerful art, literature, poetry, activism, and social change. I think the center and the library do an excellent job of ensuring the legacy of gay and lesbian history while promoting cross-cultural dialogue and chronicling LGBT culture for future generations.

Jan Zivic: Unfortunately, the center's proud and very public outing of gay and lesbian culture has also resulted in some acts of violence at the library. I remember the destruction of library books that resulted in the *Reversing Vandalism* show that Jim Van Buskirk put together. It was incredible; the artists transformed the books that had been vandalized into works of art.

catalogue. We found, ultimately, six hundred defaced volumes—on women's health issues, HIV and AIDS, and gay and lesbian issues—and when we got them back from the police we offered them to visual artists to explore as art. Unfortunately we have had other incidents of vandalism at the library and the center. There was one incident in which the letters "HIV" were carved inside elevator cabins and another in which a vandal carved the words "Kill Faggots" on a table in the Hormel Center. It was a low point but it was actually a high point at the same time, because it was the perfect demonstration of why the center is so important. I thought, "This is why we're doing this. This is why we've spent all this energy. We still have a long way to go." I think the fact that this book is being published by the San Francisco Public Library—one of the first that they have published—is a testimony to the pioneering efforts of the community and the staff of this institution. I was speaking recently with my colleague who directs the Filipino collection at the San Francisco Public Library, and she said, "Wow, I am so impressed with what you all are doing. It makes me think that I should do this for my center as well." It just keeps going.

Barbara Levine: The common goals and dedication shine through and largely account for the success of the Hormel Center; the fact that you're all here today and interested in the next chapter of the center's history speaks volumes on what great civic and community partnerships can accomplish. It is an honor and a pleasure to be here with you all and to work on this project. It's a marvelous feat to have the center and to have it be so vital and to know that the goal of having a legacy is actually happening.

Chuck Forester: I'd like to make a concluding comment. We get a lot of credit for being such good fundraisers ... but this center wouldn't be here if it wasn't for this library. Not just physically. The library staff did an incredible job in putting together the collection and nurturing the idea from its first beginnings as the "gay Schomburg" concept to the endowed public space that it is today. You can't think of the San Francisco Public Library without thinking of the Hormel Center. It's one of the jewels in the crown of our library—and our city.

RIGHT:
Hormel Center view
Into the Light mural

Into the Light

The Hormel Center Mural

Into the Light is the trompe l'oeil mural created by Mark Evans and Charley Brown especially for the ceiling of the James C. Hormel Gay and Lesbian Center. The design evolved over a year and a half, and the execution involved a process rarely used in the United States, in which canvas is covered with a mix of marble dust and polymers to create a smooth, plasterlike surface, over which aluminum leaf is applied. Working in their San Francisco studio from November 1995 to March 1996, the artists focused on one semicircular canvas at a time, using a thick, viscous brown paint and employing a variety of techniques involving rags, hands, and thousands of cotton swabs to achieve the mural's luminous shades of burnt umber on silver leaf. The two halves of the circular canvas, a total of 22 feet in diameter, were rolled out and affixed to the center's ceiling on March 13, 1996.

The mural is allegorical, depicting a construction site in which men, women, and children work together to move from the darkness of ignorance into the light of knowledge. The artists photographed friends and colleagues to use as models, and then altered the figures, rendering them largely unrecognizable. The only figures intended to be identifiable are those of Ambassador James C. Hormel, for whom the center is named, and Asye and Robert Kenmore, whose generosity made the mural possible. The blocks comprising the structure bear the names of prominent historical figures from various countries and time periods known to have had same-sex relationships. The names were chosen by the artists from lists compiled by the Gay Lesbian Bisexual Task Force of the American Library Association and made available by the staff of the San Francisco Public Library.

Names from the Hormel Center mural

Aristotle (384-322 B.C.E.), Athenian philosopher

Alexander the Great (356-323 B.C.E.), Macedonian ruler

Ovid (Publius Ovidius Naso, 43 B.C.E.-C.E. 18), Roman poet

Hadrian (Publius Aelius Hadrian, C.E. 76-138), Roman ruler

Richard I (The Lion Heart, 1157-1199), British ruler

Rumi (Jelal al-Din, 1207-1273), Persian poet, mystic

Hafiz (Shams ud-Din Mohammed, d. 1389?), Persian poet

Donatello (Donato di Niccolo di Betto Bardo, 1386-1466), Italian sculptor

Leonardo Da Vinci (1452-1519), Italian artist, inventor

Vasco de Gama (1460-1524), Portuguese admiral, explorer

Niccolo Machiavelli (1469-1527), Italian statesman

Michelangelo Buonarroti (1475-1564), Italian artist

Raphael (Raphael Santi, 1483-1520), Italian artist

Correggio (Antonio Allegri Correggio, 1494-1534), Italian artist

Suleiman I (1494-1566), Turkish sultan

Cellini (Benvenuto Cellini, 1500-1571), Italian sculptor, writer

Caravaggio (Michelangelo Merisi da Caravaggio, 1569-1609), Italian artist

Frederick the Great (1712-1786), Prussian ruler

Mary Wollstonecraft (1759-1797), British writer

Walt Whitman (1819-1892), U.S. poet

Florence Nightingale (1820-1910), British nurse, reformer

Karl Ulrichs (1825-1895), German lawyer, sociologist, reformer

Emily Dickinson (1830-1886), U.S. poet

Seiku Okuhara (1837-1913), Japanese poet

Peter Ilyich Tchaikovsky (1840-1893), Russian composer

We'Wha (1849-1896), Two-Spirit, Zuni weaver, potter

Oscar Wilde (1856-1900), Irish writer

Magnus Hirschfeld (1868-1935), German sociologist

Marcel Proust (1871-1922), French writer

Willa Cather (1873-1947), U.S. writer

Into the Light mural

Colette (Sidonie-Gabrielle Colette Goudeket, 1873-1954), French writer

Gertrude Stein (1874-1946), U.S.-born writer, patron of the arts

Isadora Duncan (1877-1927), U.S. choreographer, dancer

Wanda Landowska (1879-1959), Polish musician

Aaron Copland (1900-1991), U.S. composer

Christopher Isherwood (1904-1986), English-born U.S. writer

Frida Kahlo (1907-1954), Mexican painter

W.H. Auden (Wystan Hugh Auden, 1907-1973), British poet, critic, scholar

Jean Genet (1910-1986), French writer

Bayard Rustin (1910-1987), U.S. political activist

Francis Bacon (1910-1992), Irish-born British painter

Tennessee Williams (1911-1985), U.S. playwright

Benjamin Britten (1913-1977), British composer

Carson McCullers (1917-1967), U.S. writer

James Baldwin (1924-1988), U.S. writer

Yukio Mishima (Kimitake Hiraoka, 1925-1970), Japanese writer

Lorraine Hansberry (1930-1965), U.S. playwright

Harvey Milk (1930-1978), U.S. politician, political activist

Manuel Puig (1932-1990), Argentine writer

Audre Lorde (1934-1992), U.S. writer

Reinaldo Arenas (1943-1990), Cuban-born U.S. writer

In October 1991, a press conference in the San Francisco History Room at the former main San Francisco Public Library announced the creation of a gay and lesbian center. At the event, Mayor Art Agnos, Library Commission President Steve Coulter, and others spoke eloquently for the importance of such a repository—believed to be the first such center in a public library in the United States. Among the collections announced were author Randy Shilts's personal papers, as well as the archival materials of Peter Adair, director of the pioneering documentary *Word is Out* and Rob Epstein and Jeffrey Friedman, responsible for *The Times of Harvey Milk* and *Common Threads: Stories from the Quilt*. As an interested staff member, I stood at the back of the crowded room listening to various civic leaders express their commitment to the concept. At the time, I had no idea how deeply the project would shape the city, the library, and my own personal and professional life.

Reflections:
Stewarding the Collections
Jim Van Buskirk

My direct involvement with the project began a few months later when Kathy Page, chief of facilities development, invited me to accompany her to Tallahassee, Florida to visit Barbara Grier and Donna McBride. The library had an opportunity to acquire their impressive collection, and Kathy wanted assistance (and perhaps a male perspective) in appraising the materials. I was eager to investigate the collection of the venerable bibliographer, reviewer, collector, and editor of the *Ladder*. Together with Donna McBride, a former reference librarian, Grier cofounded Naiad Press, America's foremost publisher of lesbian books. Kathy Page and I spent several days inventorying rooms full of materials, including business records, correspondence, and publications of Naiad Press, as well as pulp paperbacks

Robert Giard
***Jim Van Buskirk*, 2000**
Gelatin silver print
Printed in 2001
ROBERT GIARD
PHOTOGRAPHS COLLECTION

and other published books amassed over the years. Letters from well-known lesbian authors like Patricia Highsmith, Jane Rule, and Ann Bannon, as well as files labeled "Lesbian Nuns controversy" made the collection rich and desirable. Kathy Page and I returned home, wrote our report, and shortly thereafter learned that the collection would be coming to the San Francisco Public Library, eventually forming the cornerstone of the gay and lesbian center's collections.

In December of 1992, I was honored to be named the first director of the center. As I surveyed the library's materials relating to LGBT experience, it became apparent that many important titles had never been acquired or were missing. Having served on the community advisory board for the gay and lesbian collection at the Eureka Valley/Harvey Milk Memorial Branch in the mid-1980s, I was well aware of the strengths of that branch's circulating collection, and the connection between the collection and the neighborhood. The new gay and lesbian center at the main library, however, was primarily envisioned as a research archives, a noncirculating collection that would document all aspects of gay, lesbian, bisexual, and transgender experience. The collection was to be national and international in scope, with its focus on Northern California.

Many individuals worked tirelessly to develop the plans, procedures, and policies that made the center a success: from library administrators, library staff at every level and throughout the entire system, and many devoted volunteers. From 1991 until 1996, the center's scope was defined and honed. Challenging issues such as how the archives' diverse media would be housed and made accessible to the public were tackled. It was difficult at first to envision exactly who would be using the archives, and in what ways. As a public institution, the library was committed to meeting the needs of anyone seeking information about LGBT experience. Materials were acquired for the adult, teen, and children's collections in a variety of formats including books, magazines and newspapers, directories, manuscripts, photographs, films, video and audio recordings. Particular attention was paid to documenting the experiences of people of color, the disabled, youth, the elderly, and other groups sometimes marginalized within the LGBT community.

One memorable challenge was negotiating the contract with the Gay and Lesbian Historical Society of Northern California. Many meetings over several years were required to establish a mutually agreeable policy whereby a selection of the society's archival holdings would be physically transferred to the library. This agreement between the community-based archives and a city agency, in which the society retains ownership while the library provides storage and staffing, remains in effect a decade later. Indicative of the lengthy process, at the beginning of the negotiations Susan Goldstein was one of the representatives of the society; by the time the contract was signed, she had been named city archivist at the San Francisco Public Library.

A decade later, the Hormel Center's archives continue to grow. The center regularly purchases published books and periodicals, and it has acquired important photographic portfolios by artists such as Cathy Cade, Daniel Nicoletta, and Robert Giard. Sometimes donors offer materials they must dispose of immediately for personal or estate reasons. Other times, a donor's understated offer reveals rare and invaluable materials about

WHY I WROTE FROM VIOLENT MEN

by Daniel Curzon

I didn't reallly know Harvey Milk. I met him at a conference in Fresno in 1975 before he was widely known. He seemed dynamic and sexy. Once on Castro Street, years later, I accepted a flyer Harvey was handing out. That was the extent of my contact with him, except as he became a political force.

When he was killed, I was driving home from teaching a class at the Catholic University of San Francisco, a class where I had to be very cautious about what I said or implied about my sexual orientation since that university discriminated against gays, and still does, following Catholic Church policy. I was devastated by the news of his death. It meant that gay rights were going to be killed too, perhaps.

On May 21, 1979 I was at City Hall following the court decision that gave Dan White a mere seven years and eight months for murdering Harvey Milk and Mayor George Moscone. I certainly incited the rioters even if I didn't actually throw any rocks. I ran with the crowds, got tear gas in my eyes, and cheered when the police cars went up in flames, their sirens howling like prehistoric beasts. I must say it was one of the most exciting nights of my life.

My rage had grown from these events as well as from a lifetime of being a "queer," the outsider. Society kept on saying that only "real men" mattered, and that anything "real men" did to "queers" was fine. Dan White was a "real man."

About 1980 I conceived a novel about an attempt to assassinate a character similar to Dan White while he was still in prison. What I was really doing was dramatizing in the Machiavellian politician and the gay [illegible] the two sides of myself as concerns the use of violence to achieve one's ends.

Daniel Curzon
Hand-edited manuscript, 1988
DANIEL CURZON PAPERS

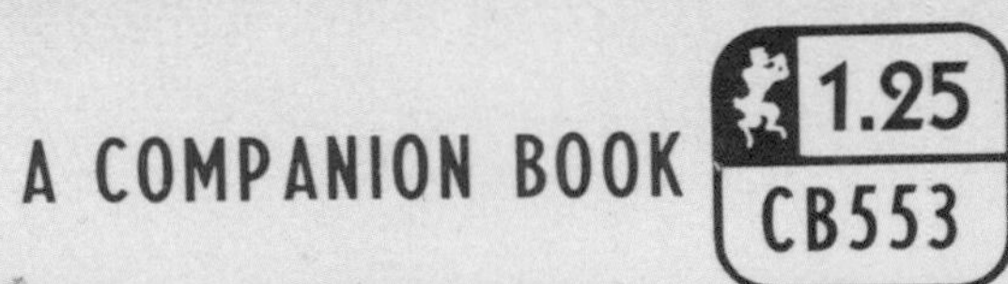

A COMPANION BOOK
1.25
CB553
ADULT READING
HE WON THE GAY VOTE BY A SINSLIDE!
SENATOR SWISH
BY ARRON THOMAS

significant individuals and organizations. Occasionally, artists and individuals—such as Jewelle Gomez—donate their papers while they are still actively creating, providing researchers unprecedented access to their work. Some archival collections contain ephemeral items such as matchbooks, buttons, T-shirts, posters, trophies, and fliers. The Hormel Center welcomes inquiries regarding all types of material; we help guide donors to appropriate repositories, whether at the library or elsewhere.

In addition to collecting, preserving, and providing access to LGBT materials, another crucial aspect of the center is its exhibitions and public programs, often achieved in collaboration with other library departments, community organizations, and individuals. There have also been many successful joint projects with affinity centers within the library such as the African American Center, the Deaf Services Center, and the Government Information Center. Exhibitions and public programs have also been cosponsored with local organizations such as the University of California at Berkeley, the Harvey Milk Institute, FTM International, and the Intersex Society of North America. Through collaborations with various organizations and individuals, I have been privileged to come to know so many members of our diverse communities. Their generosity, commitment, and vision continue to shape the direction of the Hormel Center's archives, public programming, and exhibitions.

Out at the Library provides an opportunity to make visible the Hormel Center's archival holdings, offering these rich treasures to the world. Many of the objects—catalogued and accessible through a variety of print and electronic formats—only see the light of day when researchers make specific requests to use them. And individuals do, on a daily basis, request archival materials for their books, documentary films, and other important projects. Students use published books, magazines, videos, and databases to study various aspects of homosexuality, or to write papers analyzing current issues such as gays in the military or same-sex marriages. I've learned that everyone moves through the world in their own fashion, processing information differently. Where one individual might prefer the written word, another is more at ease with the moving image. The Hormel Center seeks to be sensitive to these issues, even acknowledging that a person might not be comfortable crossing the threshold into the center's beautiful, ceremonial space. For this reason, materials in a variety of formats are housed throughout the library system. As Judy Grahn's powerful essay reminds us, individual lives leave tracks. Collected, these tracks begin to tell stories of who we are, who we were, and who we have dreams of becoming. In a society that often wants to erase our existence, preserving these tracks and making them accessible in a safe place can sometimes save lives.

Which brings me, in closing, to a memory that I would like to share. In the midst of readying the center for the grand opening in April 1996, there were many details to oversee. By the time we opened the doors, staff members were exhausted. I remember during that first exhilarating week sitting in the Hormel Center, observing people using the center. A teenage boy working on one of the computers seemed to be having trouble. When I approached him to offer assistance, he waved me away. This happened a few times before he left the room. He soon reappeared and asked me to help him find a book that he could check out.

LEFT:
Arron Thomas
Senator Swish
San Diego, CA:
Phenix Publishers ltd.,
1968

Rick Gerharter
Nurse Isabel McCoy hugs Rita Rocket as she serves dessert at her monthly brunch in Ward 5A, the AIDS ward at San Francisco General Hospital
1992
Gelatin silver print
RICK GERHARTER PHOTOGRAPHS COLLECTION

What kind of book did he want, I asked. "A book about gays—like me," he said. In the course of looking for a book together, he told me that he couldn't talk about his situation to the other kids at his Catholic school. I started to commiserate when he cut me off, explaining that he could talk to the lesbian next door. When I handed him a book (*Am I Blue? Coming Out from the Silence*, edited by Marion Dane Bauer), his first question was, "If I check this out, will my parents find out?" He seemed reassured to learn that library circulation records remained confidential. "That's good," he said. "It would kill them if they knew I was gay." Then he asked for information about a social service agency where he could find counseling. I was impressed by the pluckiness of this fellow who looked about thirteen, and the fact that he even knew the term "social service agency." When I gave him the phone number for the Lavender Youth Recreation and Information Center, he asked for something in the East Bay, where he lived. As I looked up the number for the Pacific Center in Berkeley, he realized, "I guess I can take BART to the Castro; I took BART to get here." Armed with his book, and the information that I had given him, he turned to go. Then he returned, and said: "I just want you to know that I'm glad you're here to help people like me." As I watched him walk away, tears filled my eyes. This was why so many people had worked so hard to create a sacred space for research and study.

Invited to speak at various library and PFLAG (Parents, Families, and Friends of Lesbians and Gays) meetings, I often recount this story, my voice cracking and my eyes tearing on each occasion. A few years after I encountered this amazing young man, I was working at the reference desk not far from the Hormel Center, when a young man approached me. "Hi, remember me?" he asked jauntily. "I'm the guy you helped find a book about gays a few years ago. I just wanted to let you know that I'm doing fine. I came out to my parents, and I'm out at school and, well, that's why I'm here, I need your help again. I'm doing a presentation to my class about homosexuality, and I want to find..." As I helped him with his research, I confessed to him that I'd been sharing his story, and I thanked him for returning to give me an update. After he left, I again reflected upon the ways in which libraries do change lives.

EXPLORING THE ARCHIVES

Hormel Center archives object and file storage

Selections from the Hormel Center Collections

Hormel Center Archives Subject and Name Index

While standardized subject headings are used in the online catalogue entries to access published material, natural language is used in the library's in-house index to archival materials. This maximizes researchers' ability to find library materials. For a discussion of the changes in standardized subject headings over time and the social and political implications of these shifts, see page 57.

A sample of the natural language index appears on the facing page. After each entry there are numbers in normal and/or bold typeface. For example, under Milk, Harvey: **19, 20, 35,** 36, the numbers refer to the call numbers of those archival collections containing information about Harvey Milk as a subject. GLC 35 is the Harvey Milk Archives—Scott Smith Collection. Since Milk himself was the source of that material, the number is bold. GLC 36 Daniel Nicoletta Photographs Collection contains images of Harvey Milk, but because Milk did not create these images the number 36 is in normal typeface.

Additional subject and name access is available through the library's online catalogue: www.sfpl.org

Hormel Center archives: boxes containing Dr. Mary Walker's boots

INDEX VERSION
FEBRUARY 2005

Daniel Nicoletta
Dressing Room, Finocchio's (transvestite revue during last week of performances)
November 20, 1999
Gelatin silver print
DANIEL NICOLETTA PHOTOGRAPHS COLLECTION

Public and Private Worlds

Who we are and what we do in our private lives may sometimes be at odds with how we live in the world, and vice versa. Imagine Dr. Mary Walker, who, at her 1856 wedding to another surgeon, wore trousers and a man's coat and kept her own name. After being appointed assistant surgeon during the American Civil War, Walker made herself a slightly modified officer's uniform to wear, in response to the demands of traveling with the soldiers and working in field hospitals. In 1865 she was the only woman ever to receive the Congressional Medal of Honor, the highest military award given by the United States. Consider also the intimate relationship of Gertrude Stein and Alice B. Toklas, a relationship that is increasingly celebrated as it becomes more public. There are a myriad of thought-provoking stories acknowledging the boundaries between private and public.

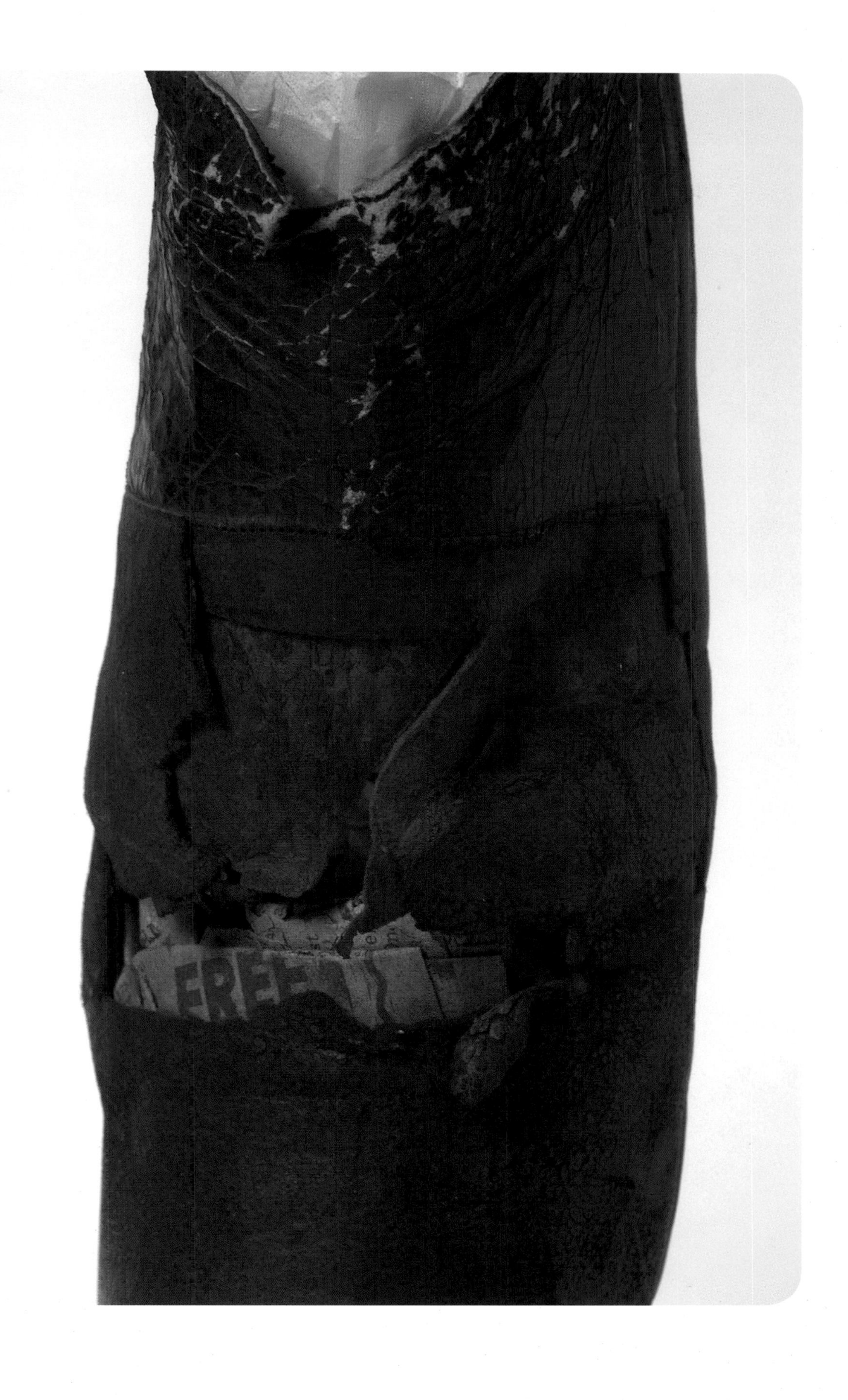

Maker unknown
Detail of boots worn by Dr. Mary Walker, c.1863
Leather, wood
BARBARA GRIER AND DONNA MCBRIDE/NAIAD PRESS COLLECTION

Dr. Mary Walker

A pair of worn leather boots, an old photograph, a postcard, and a newspaper clipping tell the story of a unique nineteenth-century figure, Dr. Mary Walker. Mary Edwards Walker (1832-1919) was the first female surgeon in the U.S. Army, a humanitarian and early advocate for women's rights, including dress reform. During the Civil War, she risked her life in her devotion to the care of the sick and wounded. Her image and life story spark the contemporary imagination, and resonated with Barbara Grier, editor of the *Ladder* and founder of Naiad Press, who collected these objects and donated them to the Hormel Center archives.

Walker was born in rural New York into an abolitionist family. In 1855 she became one of the earliest female physicians upon graduation from Syracuse Medical College. Wearing trousers and a dress-coat, she married another physician, Albert Miller, in a ceremony that did not include a promise to obey. Throughout her marriage she was known as Mary Walker, foregoing the tradition of taking her husband's name. She and her husband set up a joint medical practice, but the public was not ready to accept a woman physician, and the practice failed. Their marriage lasted thirteen years, ending in divorce.

When war broke out, Dr. Walker tried to join the Union Army. Denied a commission as a medical officer, she volunteered as a field surgeon. Two years later, she finally won a commission as an army surgeon. Dr. Walker modified an officer's uniform to wear as she traversed the battlefields. She continually crossed enemy lines to care for civilians and it is generally accepted that she worked as a Union spy during this period. Captured by Confederate troops in 1864, she was imprisoned for four months until she was released in a prisoner exchange. After the war, Dr. Walker became a writer and lecturer, touring the United States and abroad. She spoke passionately on behalf of women's rights, dress reform, health care, and temperance.

Taking pride in her numerous arrests for wearing full male dress, Dr. Walker continued to wear men's clothes exclusively for the rest of her life. Dr. Walker received the Congressional Medal of Honor in an order signed by President Andrew Johnson in 1865. The government revoked 900 such medals from civilian recipients in 1917, and asked for Walker's medal back. She refused the government's request, wearing the medal every day until her death. In 1977 President Jimmy Carter reinstated her medal posthumously.

LEFT TO RIGHT, TOP TO BOTTOM:
Photographer unknown
***Dr. Mary Walker*, c.1863**
Gelatin silver print

Maker unknown
Boots worn by Dr. Mary Walker
c.1863
Leather, wood

Helaine Victoria Press
Postcard of Dr. Mary Walker
Postmarked 1975

ALL MATERIALS:
BARBARA GRIER AND DONNA MCBRIDE/NAIAD PRESS COLLECTION

Gertrude Stein and Alice B. Toklas

Gertrude Stein (1874-1946) and Alice B. Toklas (1877-1967) have iconic status in the history of both twentieth-century literature and lesbian culture. Raised in Oakland and San Francisco respectively, the two women met in Paris in 1907. Stein sought to revitalize language and connect it with inner experience, to articulate consciousness through abstract, repetitive, rhythmical texts evoking "the excitingness of pure being." With her brother Leo Stein, she amassed one of the first collections of avant-garde painting, with an emphasis on Cubism. By the 1920s, Stein and Toklas's home at 27 Rue de Fleurus became the site of a salon frequented by the most significant artists and writers of the time, notably Henri Matisse, Pablo Picasso, Georges Braque, Juan Gris, Marsden Hartley, F. Scott Fitzgerald, Ernest Hemingway, Sherwood Anderson, and Paul Bowles. The resonance between Stein's writing and the experiments of the Cubist painters was at the heart of the convivial, intellectually vibrant gatherings. Stein coined the term "lost generation" to describe some of the writers, and her judgments on art and literature were profoundly influential. While Stein held forth among the men, Toklas, known for her culinary skills, led the women away to chat about food and fashion.

new situation in so traditional a manner that they as it - or both are lost. After all their pioneers now have to be in the arts or sciences and that is wonderful for those who are of these activities but not so wonderful for those outside them. I hope you are going on your way cheerfully -

I was so pleased to hear of your grandmother and your Aunt Alice - please give them both my warmest remembrances - they are both a particularly vivid picture to me - perhaps because of their being so handsome - carrying themselves superbly and their strong resemblance - your aunt Alice promised to become what her mother was - Family resemblances fascinate me. Do you get your Eric's resemblance from your mother? -

With many thanks and a kind remembrance

I am always cordially yours

Alice Toklas.

Why not ask your French girl friend to come and see me - She of the umbrella and the Autobiography?

exp. Toklas. 5 rue Christine VI Paris.

Par Avion.

Donald Frank Esquire.
2822 North West Cumberland Road.
Portland.
Oregon.
Etats-Unis.

NANCY - PLACE STANISLAS
25
PARIS-TRI DEPART

LEFT TO RIGHT:
Horst
***Gertrude Stein at Pierre Balmain fashion show*, 1946**
Gelatin silver print
Reproduction

Alice B. Toklas
Letter to Donald H. Frank
1947
ALICE B. TOKLAS COLLECTION OF LETTERS TO DONALD H. FRANK

5 rue Christine VI Paris.

23-I-48.

Dear Donald-

Your letter has remained unanswered because there were numbers of things that needed immediate attention and everything else had to be thrust aside. But your letter interested me a lot. You have accepted the present difficulties with less resistance than most of the young men who write to me - not because you are satisfied with conditions but because you realise Horace Greeley's to resume is to resume. Gertrude Stein kept telling the returning soldiers that they would have to become pioneers again - not on the soil but within themselves - And you have the advantage of finding your daily work to be not only for yourself but for your family - an obligation not a sacrifice - than which there is nothing more degrading and for both sides - for the one making it and for those for whom it is made. On that score you are fortunate.

As for world peace - there is no such bird - There is no peace on earth - on earth Gertrude Stein said in Four Saints - and it wasn't just poetry to her. En passant her work was all based on what she profoundly believed - the music - as she called it - though inherent was incidental. As the world grows smaller and moves more quickly - it is even possible that peace is

Toklas managed the couple's domestic life and meticulously proofread and typed all of Stein's manuscripts. Several rare Stein works are housed in the library's Book Arts & Special Collections Center. *Two Poems* is a fine-press book printed posthumously in 1948 (with copyright by Alice B. Toklas). *A Book Concluding With As a Wife Has a Cow* is a [limited] edition facsimile of a book published in France in 1926. It was reissued in 1973, with facsimiles of the original lithographs by Juan Gris. An example of Toklas's delicate handwriting is seen in the letter to Donald H. Frank, the son of a childhood friend. The postcard, showing Gertrude and Alice at home together amidst their paintings, was sent by the poet Elsa Gidlow to her publisher Barbara Grier, of Naiad Press, in 1977.

GERTRUDE STEIN

A Book Concluding With As A Wife Has A Cow

A LOVE STORY

WITH FACSIMILES OF THE ORIGINAL LITHOGRAPHS

BY

JUAN GRIS

1973

Something Else Press · Inc.

Barton Millerton Berlin

Copyright 1948 by Alice B. Toklas

TWO

(hitherto unpublished)

POEMS

by Gertrude Stein

(now published for the first time by)

The Gotham Book Mart

New York

LEFT TO RIGHT, TOP TO BOTTOM:

Helaine Victoria Press
Postcard of Gertrude Stein and Alice B. Toklas
Postmarked 1977
BARBARA GRIER AND DONNA MCBRIDE/NAIAD PRESS COLLECTION

Gertrude Stein
A Book Concluding With As a Wife Has a Cow
Barton, VT: Something Else Press, 1973
Reprint with facsimiles of original lithographs by Juan Gris
Originally published in 1926
SCHMULOWITZ COLLECTION OF WIT & HUMOR, BOOK ARTS & SPECIAL COLLECTIONS

Alice B. Toklas
Letter to Donald H. Frank
1948
ALICE B. TOKLAS COLLECTION OF LETTERS TO DONALD H. FRANK

Gertrude Stein
Two Poems
New York: Gotham Book Mart, 1948
Printed at the Banyan Press, no. 213 of 415
GRABHORN COLLECTION ON THE HISTORY OF PRINTING, BOOK ARTS & SPECIAL COLLECTIONS

Barbara Gittings

A pioneer of the lesbian and gay rights movement since 1958, Barbara Gittings (b. 1932) is recognized for her daring, innovative strategies and inspired activism. Her groundbreaking work as an advocate for the inclusion of gay and lesbian works in public libraries is her greatest legacy.

Aware that she was "different," Gittings left her home in Wilmington, Delaware, at the age of seventeen. Socially isolated as so many young gay people are, Gittings discovered clues to her identity through library books. She ventured west to San Francisco in 1956 and became involved with the Daughters of Bilitis (DOB), the first known lesbian organization in the United States, which had been founded the previous year. In 1958, DOB encouraged Gittings to establish an East Coast chapter in Philadelphia. She did so and marched in the first gay rights demonstrations in the early 1960s, on the Fourth of July in front of Philadelphia's Independence Hall and later at the Pentagon in Washington.

Officially, the DOB had opposed picketing. "It was risky, and we were scared. Picketing was not a popular tactic at the time, and our cause seemed outlandish even to most gay people." From 1963 to 1966, Gittings served as editor of the organization's newsletter, the *Ladder*, and under her leadership it became the first movement publication to champion social protest. Gittings subtitled her publication "A Lesbian Review," and introduced photographs of gay women on the covers—bold innovations in the fight against the pervasive invisibility of gays.

In the 1970s, Gittings was in the forefront of the challenge to the American Psychiatric Association's now discredited view of homosexuality. Though not a librarian, her energy and vision became focused on libraries. From 1971 to 1986, she headed the Gay Task Force of the American Library Association (ALA), the first gay task force in any professional organization. Gittings edited "A Gay Bibliography" and gay reading lists for the task force, and recounted its history in the pamphlet "Gays in Library Land." She "starred" in the first gay kissing booth, created for the 1971 ALA conference in Dallas in order to draw attention to gay literature—and gay librarians. A media uproar ensued at the conference.

From 1998 to 2002, Gittings served on the Hormel Endowment Committee for the Hormel Center. In 2001, following the example of the Hormel Center collection, the Free Library of Philadelphia established a Gay and Lesbian collection of circulating materials at its Independence branch, and named it for Barbara Gittings—an apt tribute. And in 2003, Gittings was recognized for her contributions to libraries and librarianship with the prestigious ALA Honorary Membership, its highest honor.

Chronology of Library of Congress Subject Headings Related to LGBT Materials

GAYS IN LIBRARY LAND

The Gay and Lesbian Task Force
of the American Library Association:
The First Sixteen Years

by Barbara Gittings

"I don't see why those people are getting all the publicity when we have so many famous authors in town."

-- Librarian at 1971 American Library Association conference in Dallas, commenting on TV coverage of the Task Force on Gay Liberation's kissing booth in the exhibit hall.

A kissing booth at a librarians' convention? A gay kissing booth? What on earth were Those People up to?

Getting ourselves noticed, that's what. Making a gay presence to highlight gay issues in a setting where homosexuality wasn't typically viewed as a concern for the profession.

When the gay group in the American Library Association formed in 1970, it was the first of its kind, the first time that gay people in any professional association had openly banded together to advance the gay cause through that profession. Why didn't this happen first among gay professionals in law or religion or the behavioral sciences, the fields that had been treating homosexuality as a special concern?

It was just good luck for ALA to be the pioneer.

A year before, at ALA's annual conference, social activists had launched a new official unit of ALA, the Social Responsibilities Round Table, under whose wing self-created task forces began to tackle neglected issues in librarianship.

© Copyright 1990 by Barbara Gittings

Barbara Gittings
Gays in Library Land:
The Gay and Lesbian Task Force of
the American Library Association:
The First Sixteen Years
Philadelphia, PA: B. Gittings, 1990

Library of Congress Subject Headings related to lesbian, gay, bisexual, and transgender subject matter have historically been slow to adapt to the contemporary use of language. Because of changing attitudes toward LGBT communities, words used to describe LGBT experience have evolved slowly and inconsistently over time. To facilitate access to books being catalogued, the Hormel Center added subject headings developed by Sanford Berman at Hennepin County Public Library to supplement those used by the Library of Congress. The following is a chronology of selected terms used by the Library of Congress:

Pre-1946 – *Sexual Perversion* (still an official heading until 1969, when it was replaced by *Homosexuality* and *Lesbianism*)

1946 – *Homosexuality* becomes an official heading

1946 – *Sodomy* is used for books about the criminal aspects of homosexuality

1954 – *Lesbianism* becomes an official heading

1955 – *Homosexuality: Bisexuality and Sodomy* are added as "see references"

1969 – *Sexual Perversion* is changed to *Sexual Deviation*

1973 – "see also reference" from *Homosexuality* to *Sexual Perversion* is removed

1976 – the terms *Homosexuals* and *Homosexuals, Male* and *Lesbians* appear for the first time

1978 – *Church Work with Homosexuals; Gay Liberation Movement; Homosexuality, Male; Lesbians in Literature*; and *Unmarried Couples* are added

1985 – *Bisexuality* is added

1987 – The term *Gay* is exchanged for the previously authorized term *Homosexual*

1988 – *Homophobia* becomes an official heading

2005 – While substantial enhancements have been made, neither *Transgender* nor *Queer* are official Library of Congress headings

Barbara Grier

The Barbara Grier and Donna McBride/Naiad Press Collection was an early acquisition by the Hormel Center. The bulk of the collection was accessioned in 1992, with additions made for several years following. Grier, a lifelong lesbian bibliographer, activist, publisher, and reviewer, is outspoken about her many contributions to the development and promotion of lesbian literature.

Barbara Grier was born in 1933 in Cincinnati, Ohio, and realized that she was a lesbian at the age of twelve. Reportedly, she researched the topic at the library before announcing her conclusion to her mother. At the age of eighteen she fell in love with Helen Bennett, a librarian from Kansas City, Missouri, with whom she lived for twenty years, in what she referred to as a marriage. A collector of lesbian writings, Grier subscribed to the *Ladder*, the magazine of the Daughters of Bilitis. She began writing brief book notes for the magazine under the pen name Gene Damon. Soon, Grier was contributing articles, short stories, and full-length book reviews under various pseudonyms including Gladys Casey, Vern Niven, and HB (in honor of Helen Bennett). Some issues of the *Ladder* are comprised

From the desk of
ELSA GIDLOW

1/18/77

Desr Barbara:

Re-reading while slightly more at leisure your various communications around the holiday season, I am reminded that you will be out here in March. Please do be sure to get in touch. My telephone is (415) 388-2111. Early a.m. or after 7 p.m. best times to reach me. Sometimes, if home, may be out in the grounds and do not then hear the telephone. Am looking forward to meeting you after all these years -- and Donna too. Can you try to plan to come to a lunch? You have to come by car as I am five miles from town and bus stop. Look forward too to showing you my earthy project here.

Your LADDER books are great. Haven't read them all yet, of course, but they look very good. Very professional job of production. I love all the photos! (Was Earhart truly a Lesbian -- I suspected and hoped. She was a heroine of mine.) Why no photo of Jeannette Foster? I am told there is none in the republished "Sex Variant Women" (which I intend to buy although I do have the original.

Dolores Klaich did write me, a lovely letter, and promised a copy of her book, not yet received. I hope you understood my feelings about the Lesbian sex questionnaire. I'd like to talk to you of this when we meet. Afterthought on the Klaich book: I am in the chapter headed (I am told) "An Elder Stateswoman"! Congratulations on all your successes. Virtue does pay off -- sometimes!

Elsa

"A Woman Appeared to me" very well done. made me nostalgic for my Paris days – Cried in her circle!"

LEFT TO RIGHT, TOP TO BOTTOM:
JEB (Joan E. Biren)
***Barbara Grier*, c.1972**
Gelatin silver print
BARBARA GRIER AND DONNA MCBRIDE/NAIAD PRESS COLLECTION

Correspondence between Barbara Grier and Elsa Gidlow
1977
BARBARA GRIER AND DONNA MCBRIDE/NAIAD PRESS COLLECTION

Lynda Koolish
***Elsa Gidlow*, 1974**
Gelatin silver print
LYNDA KOOLISH PHOTOGRAPHS COLLECTION

Claire Morgan (Patricia Highsmith)
The Price of Salt
New York: Bantam Books, 1952

almost entirely of her writings. Grier also wrote for *ONE*, *Mattachine Review*, and other homophile publications. Grier worked as the *Ladder's* poetry and fiction editor from 1966 to 1968, when she assumed the general editorship. As editor, she wanted to take the journal in a more activist direction, and, in what is still considered a controversial coup, she announced that the *Ladder* was no longer associated with the Daughters of Bilitis. The *Ladder* did not prove financially viable, and ceased publication in 1972.

Inspired by Jeannette H. Foster's 1956 study, *Sex Variant Women in Literature*, Grier and Lee Stuart published *The Lesbian in Literature* in 1967—a bibliography that listed "all known books in the English language, in the general field of literature, concerned with Lesbianism, or having Lesbian characters." Grier compiled two subsequent editions of the publication in 1975 and 1981.

When Anyda Marchant approached her with the idea of publishing her first novel, *The Latecomer*, Grier was able to take advantage of her connections with the lesbian and feminist community to establish Naiad Press. Naiad Press was conceived of as a movement press—by lesbians, about lesbians, and for lesbians—with the further distinction that for every financially successful title published, there would be at least one important or scholarly work that would not break even financially. In addition to the many mysteries, romances, and science fiction novels it launched, Naiad has reprinted classics such as Patricia Highsmith's *The Price of Salt* and Ann Bannon's *Beebo Brinker* series, as well as such nonfiction titles as the controversial *Lesbian Nuns: Breaking Silence*, edited by Rosemary Curb and Nancy Manahan.

Hormel Center archives: pulp paperback collection

Pulp Paperbacks

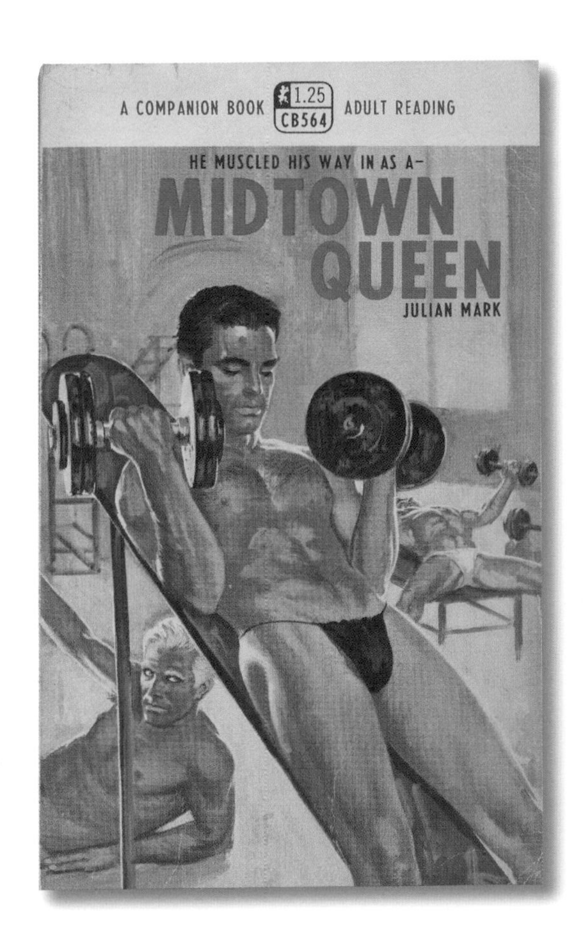

LEFT TO RIGHT:
Ross Roberts
Some Are That Way
Np: National Library Books, 1971

Julian Mark
Midtown Queen
Companion Books
San Diego, CA:
Phenix Publishers Ltd., 1968

OPPOSITE PAGE:
Kay Addams
Warped Desire
New York: Beacon, 1952

Following World War II, inexpensive paperback novels began flooding American newsstands and drugstore racks. Many of these books were sensational, not written for literary audiences, but others were well written. Many dealt with lesbian and male homosexuality. The writers—male, female, straight, gay—often used pseudonyms, and their actual readership diverged from the intended audience. With provocative titles, sexually explicit covers, lurid descriptions, and frequently tragic endings, these pulp paperbacks might be viewed as stereotypic, negative, and exploitative. However, they are probably the largest body of overtly gay writings of the time, providing information and encouragement to thousands of isolated homosexuals across the country, at least until the late 1960s, when the gay liberation movement made overt what had formerly existed underground.

These books, printed on cheap paper and disposable, were instead saved and collected by many readers. Barbara Grier's collection became an early cornerstone of the Hormel Center's collection and has been supplemented with other fragile volumes given by a wide variety of donors. Many of the Hormel Center's pulp paperbacks have been featured in exhibitions at the library, including: *Strange Sisters: The Art of Lesbian Pulp Fiction* and *Lost on Twilight Road: The Golden Age of Gay Male Pulps*. The center has also hosted public programs featuring original pulp authors Victor J. Banis and Ann Bannon, historians Susan Stryker and Michael Bronski, and artists such as F. Allen Sawyer and his Hot Pants Homo Players, who re-imagine pulps in a new context. These fanciful and subversive artifacts offer a window into an important aspect of LGBT history.

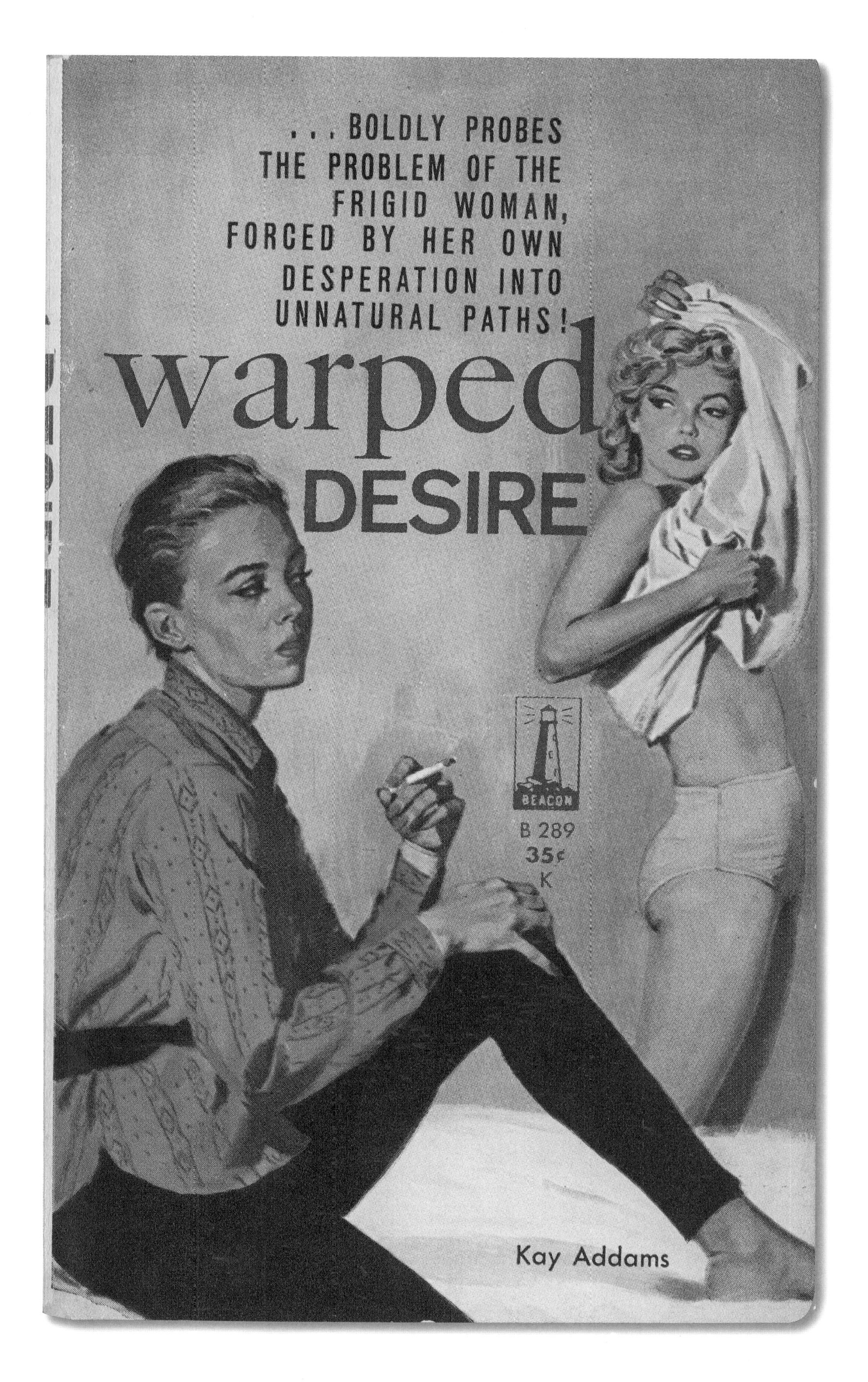
...BOLDLY PROBES
THE PROBLEM OF THE
FRIGID WOMAN,
FORCED BY HER OWN
DESPERATION INTO
UNNATURAL PATHS!
warped
DESIRE
BEACON
B 289
35¢
K
Kay Addams

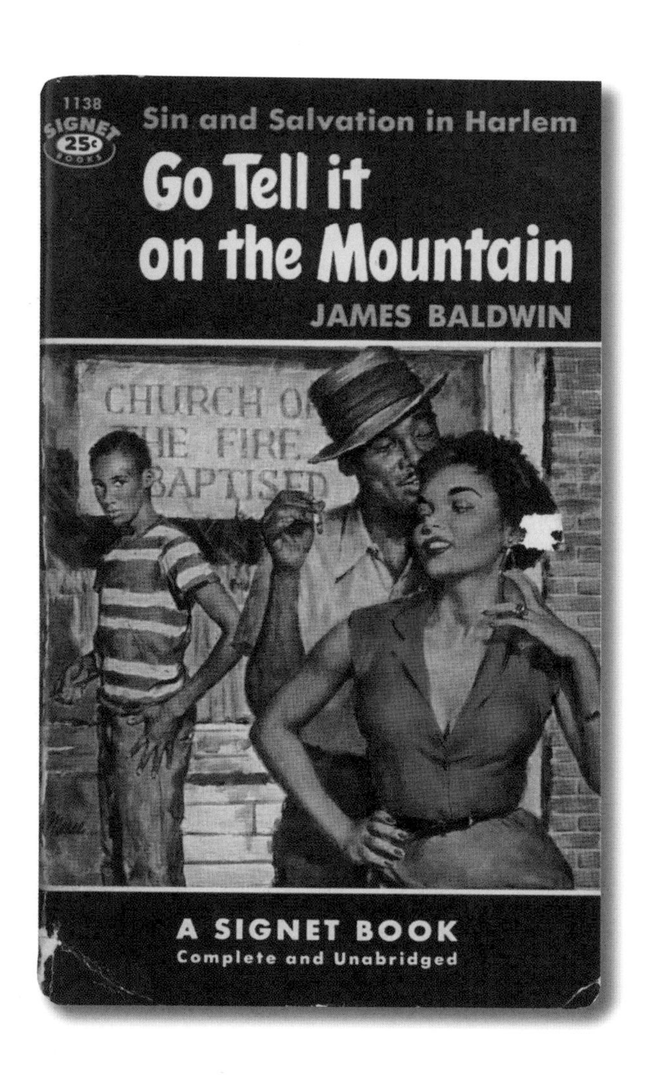

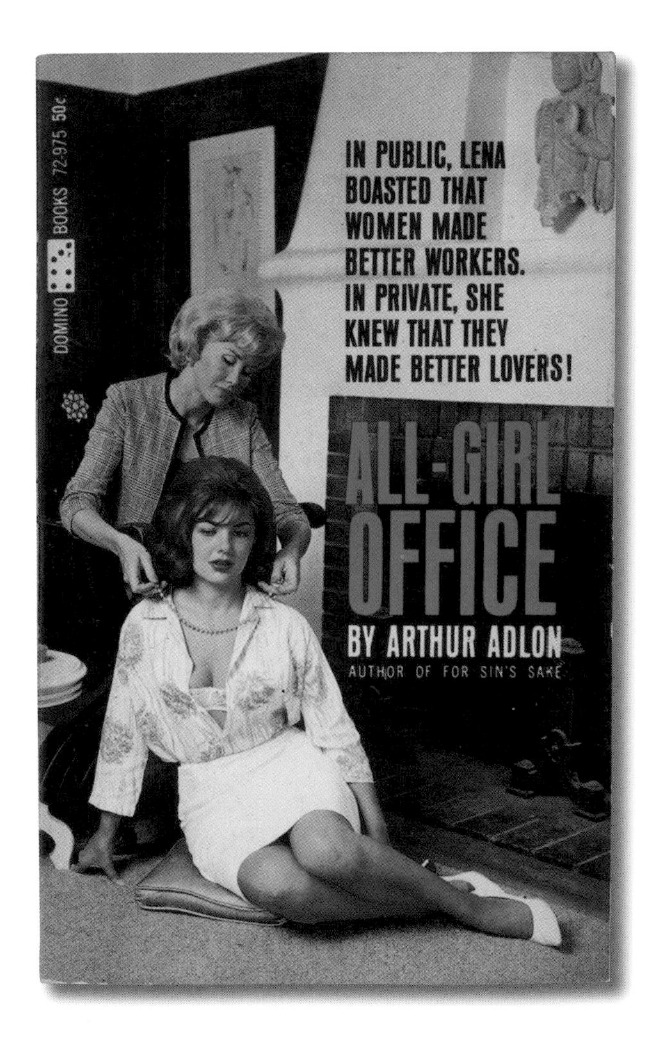

LEFT TO RIGHT, TOP TO BOTTOM:
James Baldwin
Go Tell it on the Mountain
New York: Signet, 1954

Arthur Adlon
All-Girl Office
New York: Domino Books, 1965

Ann Bannon
Odd Girl Out
New York: Fawcett, 1957

Laura Wright Brent
Lavender Love Rumble
Brentwood, CA: Brentwood Publishing, 1965

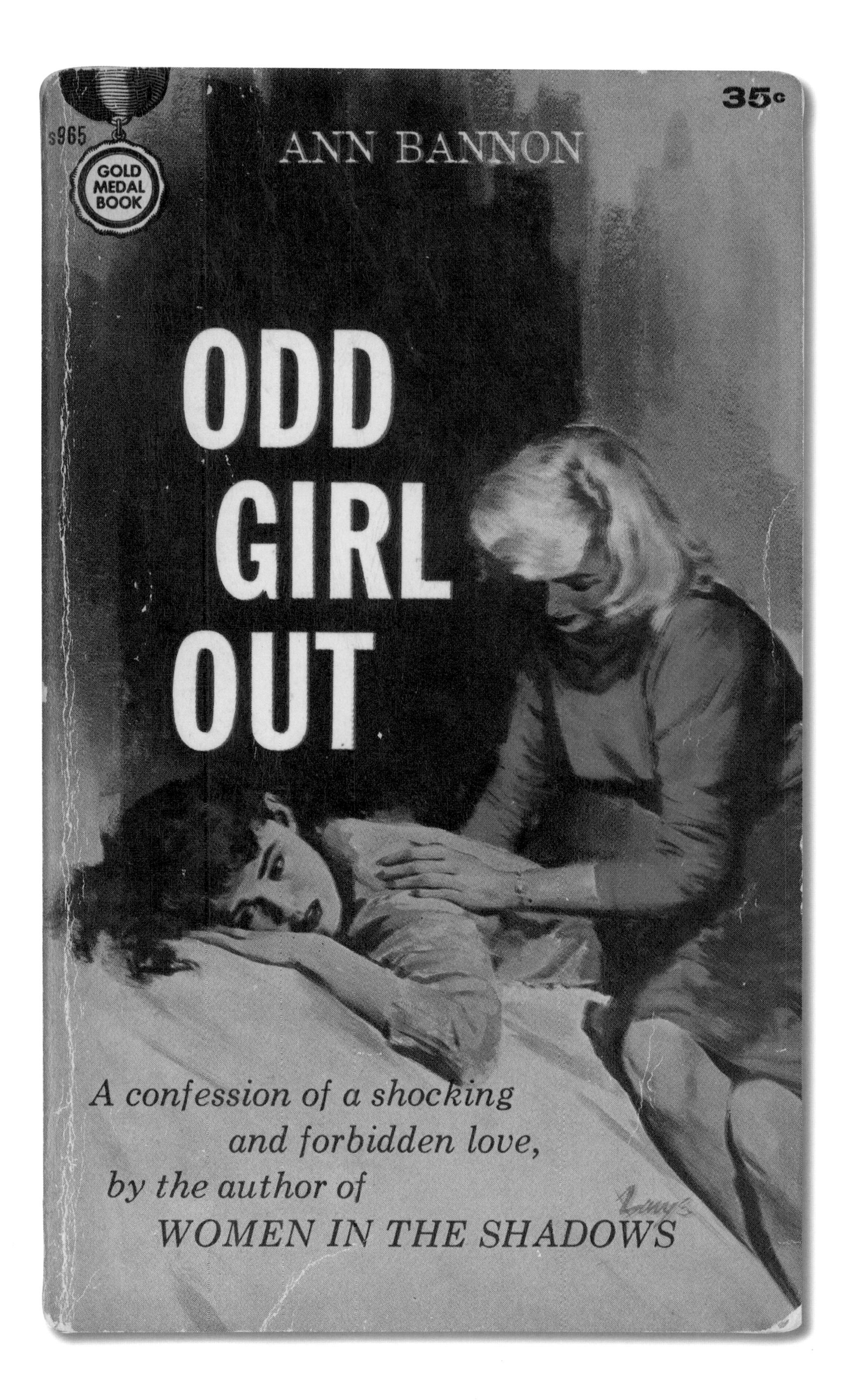
35¢
s965
GOLD
MEDAL
BOOK
ANN BANNON
ODD
GIRL
OUT
A confession of a shocking
and forbidden love,
by the author of
WOMEN IN THE SHADOWS

Pseudonyms

Pseudonyms have been especially useful for those who have had to protect themselves from arrest, physical abuse, and other forms of persecution. Karl Heinrich Ulrichs, a German law student journalist and secretary to various civil servants and diplomats, used the pseudonym Numa Numantius when he published his 1864 study *Forschungen uber das Ratsel der mannmannlichen Liebe* (Researches on the Riddle of Male-Male Love). Similarly, Karl Maria Benkert, an Austro-Hungarian man of letters, translator, and journalist, used the name Károly Mária Kertbeny to protect his family when he published the document that coined the word "homosexual."

In the 1950s and 1960s, some homophile organizations insisted that members use pseudonyms for all movement business even if they were "out" in other areas of their lives. For example, William Dorr Legg, an early contributor to *ONE,* wrote as "Valentine Richardson." Pseudonyms created the appearance that there were multiple contributors to such periodicals. Jim Kepner wrote as Frank Golovita, John Arnold, and Lyn Pedersen. The prolific Victor J. Banis wrote many novels using a wide variety of pseudonyms including: Don Holliday, J.X. Williams, Lynn Benedict, Jan Alexander, and Victor Jay.

Barbara Grier's papers contain fascinating letters with writers such as Patricia Highsmith, May Sarton, and others exchanging views on the subject of pseudonyms, the right to privacy, and the evolution of gay and lesbian identity. Some women writers continue to be known primarily by their pseudonyms: Renée Vivien was born Pauline Tarn, Marguerite Yourcenar was originally named Marguerite de Crayencour, and Mary Renault's birth name was Eileen Mary Challans. Many other writers have used both their birth names and pseudonyms at different times, including Djuna Barnes ("Lydia Steptoe"), Patricia Highsmith ("Claire Morgan"), Barbara Grier ("Gene Damon"), Jill Johnston ("F.J. Crowe"), Audre Lorde ("Rey Domini"), and Judy Grahn ("Carol Silver"). *Vice Versa*, the first lesbian periodical, was created and distributed by "Lisa Ben," an anagram for lesbian.

The following list demonstrates a small sampling of the many pseudonyms used by LGBT authors and activists.

PSEUDONYM	BIRTH NAME
Jan Addison	Jeanette Howard Foster
Sarah Aldridge	Anyda Marchant
Nathan Aldyne	Michael McDowell and Axel Young
Phil Andros	Samuel Steward
Ann Bannon	Ann Thayer
Arthur Bell	Arthur Irving
Ellen Bedoz	Ellen Shumsky
Lisa Ben	Edith Eyde
Edgar Box	Gore Vidal
Rose Brock	Joseph Hansen
Bryher	Annie Winifred Ellerman
Carpenter	June Arnold
Lee Chapman	Marion Zimmer Bradley
James Colton	Joseph Hansen
Giselle Commons	Tee Corinne
Florence Conrad	Florence Jaffy
Marie Corelli	Mary Mackay
Donald Webster Cory	Edward Sagarin
F.J. Crowe	Jill Johnston
Marvin Cutler	Dorr Legg
Gene Damon	Barbara Grier
John Dexter	Marion Zimmer Bradley
Rey Domini	Audre Lorde
Stephen Donaldson	Bob Martin
Elana Dykewomon	Elana Nachman
Alice Eliot	Sarah Orne Jewett
Hilary Farr	Jeanette Howard Foster
Ann Ferguson	Phyllis Lyon
Ronald Forsythe	Donn Teal
Miriam Gardner	Marion Zimmer Bradley
Mary Geller	Mary Wings
Meredith Gray	Marion Glass
Lily Hansen	Lili Vincenz
Cal Harding	Elver Barker
Morgan Ives	Marion Zimmer Bradley
Geraldine Jackson	Betty Perdue
William (Bill) Lambert	Dorr Legg
Elizabeth Lang	Nancy Dean
Vernon Lee	Violet Paget
Eann MacDonald	Harry Hay
Artemis March	March Hoffman
Xavier Mayne	Edward I. Stevenson

PSEUDONYM	BIRTH NAME
Maryjane Meeker	Ann Aldrich
Ralph Meeker	Forman Brown
Dick Michaels	Richard Mitch
Isabel Miller	Alma Routsong
Claire Morgan	Patricia Highsmith
Jack Nichols	Warren Adkins
Numa Numantius	Karl Heinrich Ulrichs
Robert Orville	George Platt Lynes
Parisex	Henry Gerber
Dr. Th. Ramien	Magnus Hirschfeld
Bill Rand	Bill Rau
Mary Renault	Eileen Mary Challans
Roberto Rolf	George Platt Lynes
Sagitta	John Henry Mackay
Abigail Sanford	Jeanette Howard Foster
Martha Shelley	Martha Altman*
Carol Silver	Judy Grahn
Anne Singleton	Ruth Benedict
Lydia Steptoe	Djuna Barnes
Richard Stevenson	Richard Lipez
Valerie Taylor	Velma Nacella Young
Wykeham Terris	Norman Haire
Kay Tobin	Kay Lahusen
Aaron Travis	Steven Saylor
Vega	Lloyd Jeffers
Renée Vivien	Pauline Tarn
S.P. Wonder	Elana Nachman
Marguerite Yourcenar	Marguerite de Crayencour

* Legally changed her name to her movement pseudonym

LIST FROM:
Completely Queer: The Gay and Lesbian Encyclopedia, by Steve Hogan and Lee Hudson. NY: Henry Holt & Co., 1998

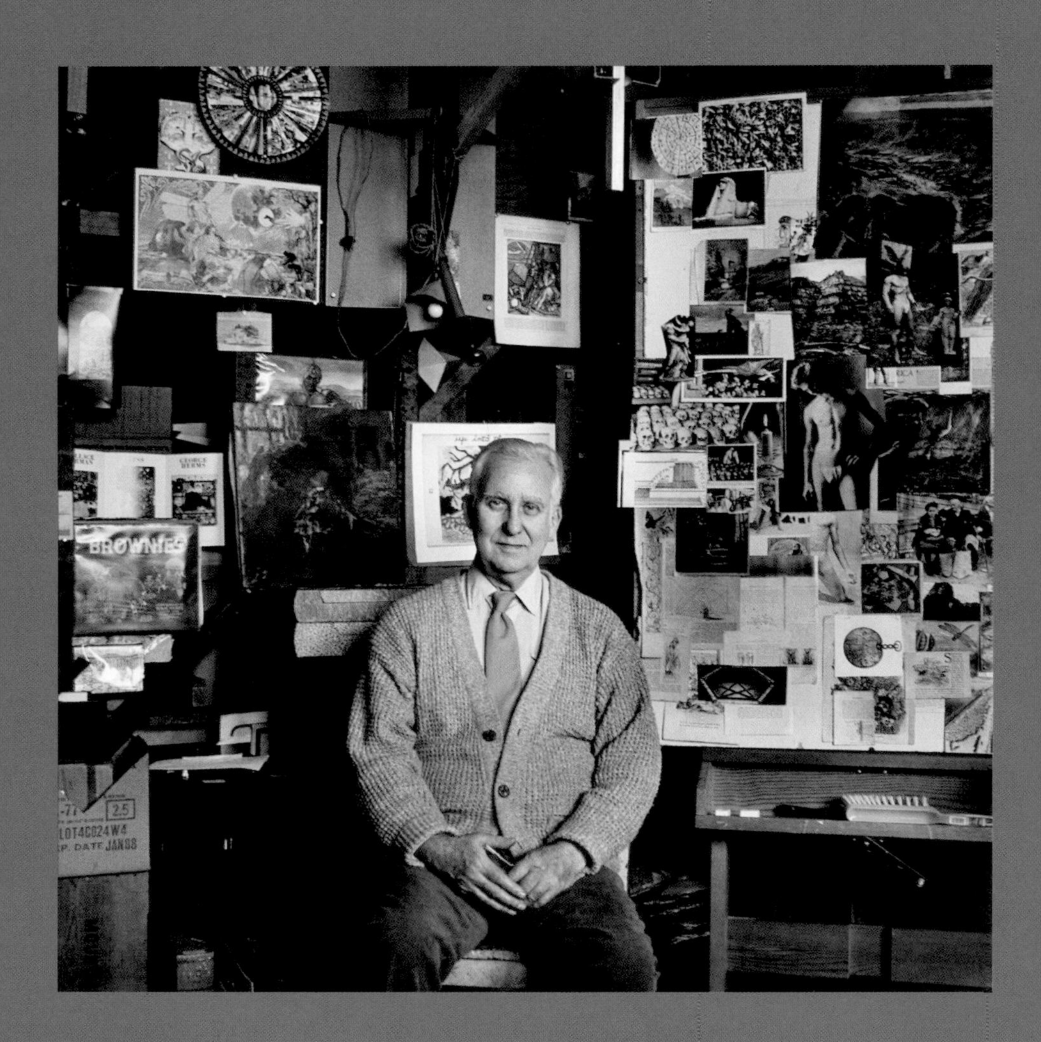

Poets and Artists

Robert Giard
Jess, 1994
Gelatin silver print
Printed in 1996
ROBERT GIARD
PHOTOGRAPHS COLLECTION

Eros—creativity, love, and the energy of life itself—speaks to us through artists and poets. We may discover the voices, insights, and experiences of LGBT individuals through their contributions to the arts—luminous connecting threads that run through history and world culture. The ability to move through different worlds, transgressing and transforming boundaries, identities, and awareness, is a skill cultivated by gays and lesbians as well as by artists and poets.

Poets have iconic stature in lesbian history and culture—beginning with the ancient Greek poet Sappho. A new poetics emerged in the confluence of 1970s feminist activism and the gay liberation movement. A vibrant network of Bay Area women poets included Judy Grahn, Elsa Gidlow, and Susan Griffin. Poetry readings were community events, electrifying rapt audiences at women's centers, bars, bookstores, and coffeehouses. Among the treasures of the Hormel archives are three original, handwritten poems by Pat Parker, donated by photographer Lynda Koolish.

In considering the history of San Francisco, compelling evidence of its bohemian, gay cultural roots emerges. A special focus on poets and artists active in the Bay Area begins with the figures of a mid-twentieth-century literary movement known as the Berkeley Renaissance or the San Francisco Renaissance. Foremost among these brilliant innovators were the poets Jack Spicer, Robin Blaser, and Robert Duncan, and the artist Jess. Rare materials related to these artists and their contemporaries are housed in the library's Book Arts & Special Collections Center. The Hormel Center also contains the archive of one of San Francisco's pioneering gay literary figures, Daniel Curzon. His novel *From Violent Men* (1983) is a gay revenge fantasy about Dan White, the convicted murderer of Supervisor Harvey Milk and Mayor George Moscone.

In the Hormel Center mural, *Into the Light*, there exist many names—spanning centuries, cultures, and creative disciplines—from Rumi to Audre Lorde. One name few people may recognize is We'Wha (1849-1896). A Zuni weaver, potter, spiritual leader, and cultural ambassador, his life exemplifies an alternative gender role recognized in many Native societies. Perceived as entwining both maleness and femaleness in one body, "Two Spirit" people were thought to be a bridge between the sexes, between the temporal and spiritual worlds. Through their special insights, creative gifts, and power, "Two Spirit" people significantly contributed to communal life as shamans, healers, singers, storytellers, and artists.

The poems and songs of Chrystos and Joy Harjo articulate emotions resulting from social injustices committed against Native Americans. With individual, political, and erotic voices, LGBT Native Americans have articulated their challenges in word and song—their strength and conviction confront us with the limitations of our culture, and their words resonate from generation to generation.

LEFT TO RIGHT, TOP TO BOTTOM:
Lynda Koolish
Jewelle Gomez, San Francisco
c.1991
Gelatin silver print
LYNDA KOOLISH
PHOTOGRAPHS COLLECTION

Lynda Koolish
Chrystos, San Francisco
OutWrite Conference, 1991
Gelatin silver print
LYNDA KOOLISH
PHOTOGRAPHS COLLECTION

Robert Giard
Blackberri, 2001
Gelatin silver print
Printed in 2002
ROBERT GIARD
PHOTOGRAPHS COLLECTION

Robert Giard
James Broughton, 1988
Gelatin silver print
Printed in 1990
ROBERT GIARD
PHOTOGRAPHS COLLECTION

LEFT TO RIGHT, TOP TO BOTTOM:
Robert Giard
Pomo Afro Homos
San Francisco, CA, 1994
Gelatin silver print
Printed in 1997
ROBERT GIARD
PHOTOGRAPHS COLLECTION

Lynda Koolish,
Robert Duncan
San Francisco, CA, c.1980
Gelatin silver print
LYNDA KOOLISH
PHOTOGRAPHS COLLECTION

Lynda Koolish
Pat Parker, 1972
Gelatin silver print
LYNDA KOOLISH
PHOTOGRAPHS COLLECTION

Poetry Books

Further exploration of the work of many of the poets represented in the Hormel Center's collections leads to the Book Arts & Special Collections Center, where rare, fine, and small-press books and little magazines are found.

In 1957, the openly gay poet Jack Spicer's "Poetry as Magic Workshop" was sponsored by the Poetry Center at San Francisco State College. The successful workshop evolved into a weekly gathering of poets, artists, university professors, and students. After a reading one night, Spicer suggested to Joe Dunn that he start a small press to publish the work of the emerging San Francisco poets. Dunn took a four-week course in printing and founded The White Rabbit Press. The first book he published was *After Lorca* by Jack Spicer, with a cover design by Jess Collins, known as Jess.

From 1957–1968, The White Rabbit Press published sixty-three books and ten broadsides. It was the primary publisher of the work of Spicer, Robin Blaser, and Robert Duncan—the three central figures of the literary movement first known as the Berkeley Renaissance, and later as the San Francisco Renaissance. *The Cat and the Blackbird*, by Robert Duncan with drawings by Jess, was published in 1967. (Duncan and Jess had met in 1951, and were a couple until Duncan's death in 1988.)

In 1952, Duncan, Jess, and the artist Harry Jacobus founded King Ubu Gallery, one of San Francisco's first alternative spaces for artists and poets. Two years later, it closed and reopened as the Six Gallery. Here, in 1955, as part of a group reading, Allen Ginsberg read in public for the first time—premiering "Howl" in an incendiary performance. The Book Arts & Special Collections Center possesses Ginsberg's work *Wichita Vortex Sutra*, published in 1966 by San Francisco's Coyote Press.

Jack Spicer
After Lorca
San Francisco: White Rabbit Press, 1957
Typed on an Olivetti Lexikon 80 by Robert Duncan and multilithed by Joe Dunn, with a cover design by Jess.
GRABHORN COLLECTION ON THE HISTORY OF PRINTING, BOOK ARTS & SPECIAL COLLECTIONS

RIGHT:
Joe Dunn
The Better Dream House
San Francisco: White Rabbit Press, 1968
With cover and 12 collages by Jess.
Limited edition of 1,000 copies.
GRABHORN COLLECTION ON THE HISTORY OF PRINTING, BOOK ARTS & SPECIAL COLLECTIONS

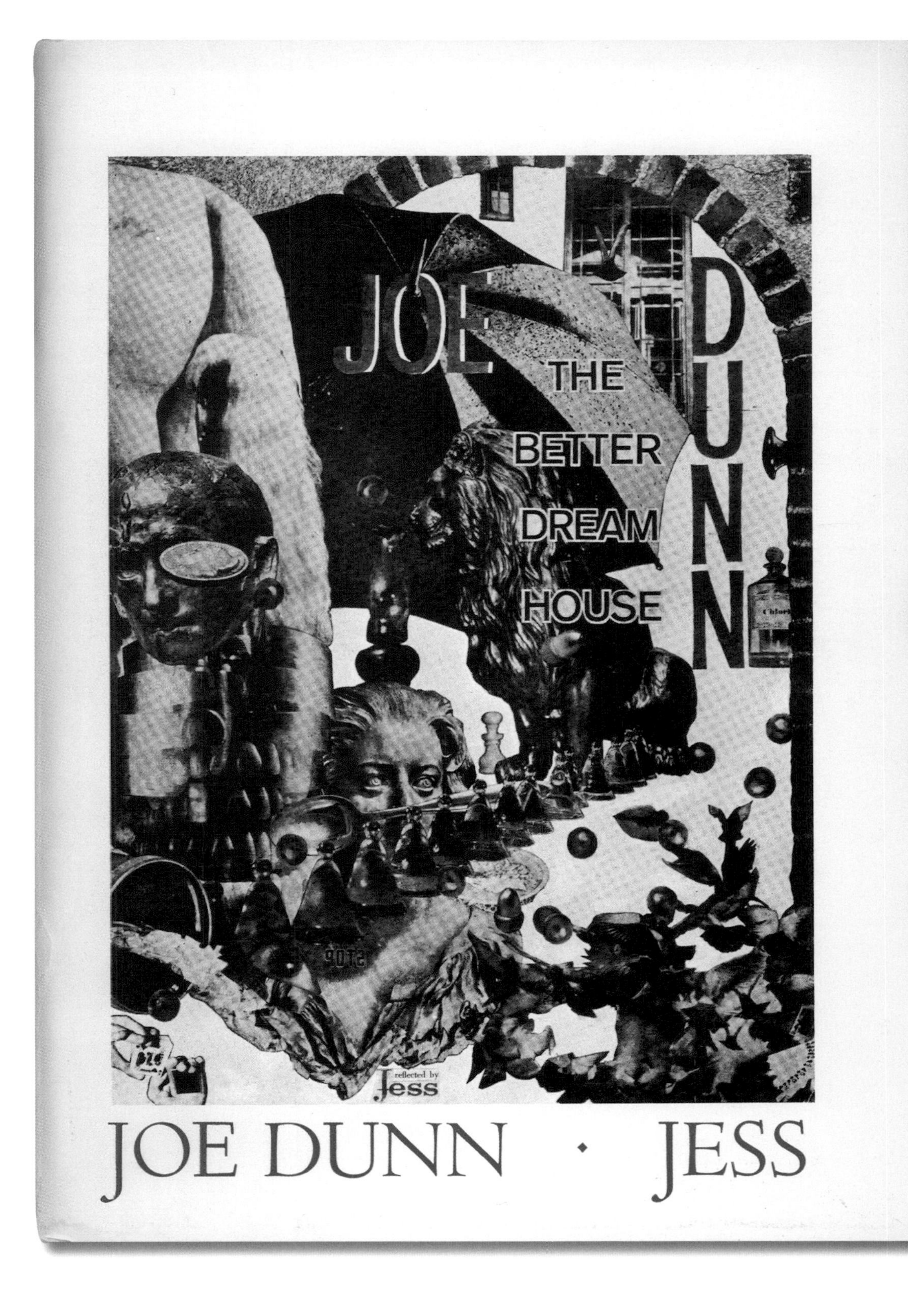
JOE
DUNN
THE
BETTER
DREAM
HOUSE
reflected by
Jess
JOE DUNN · JESS

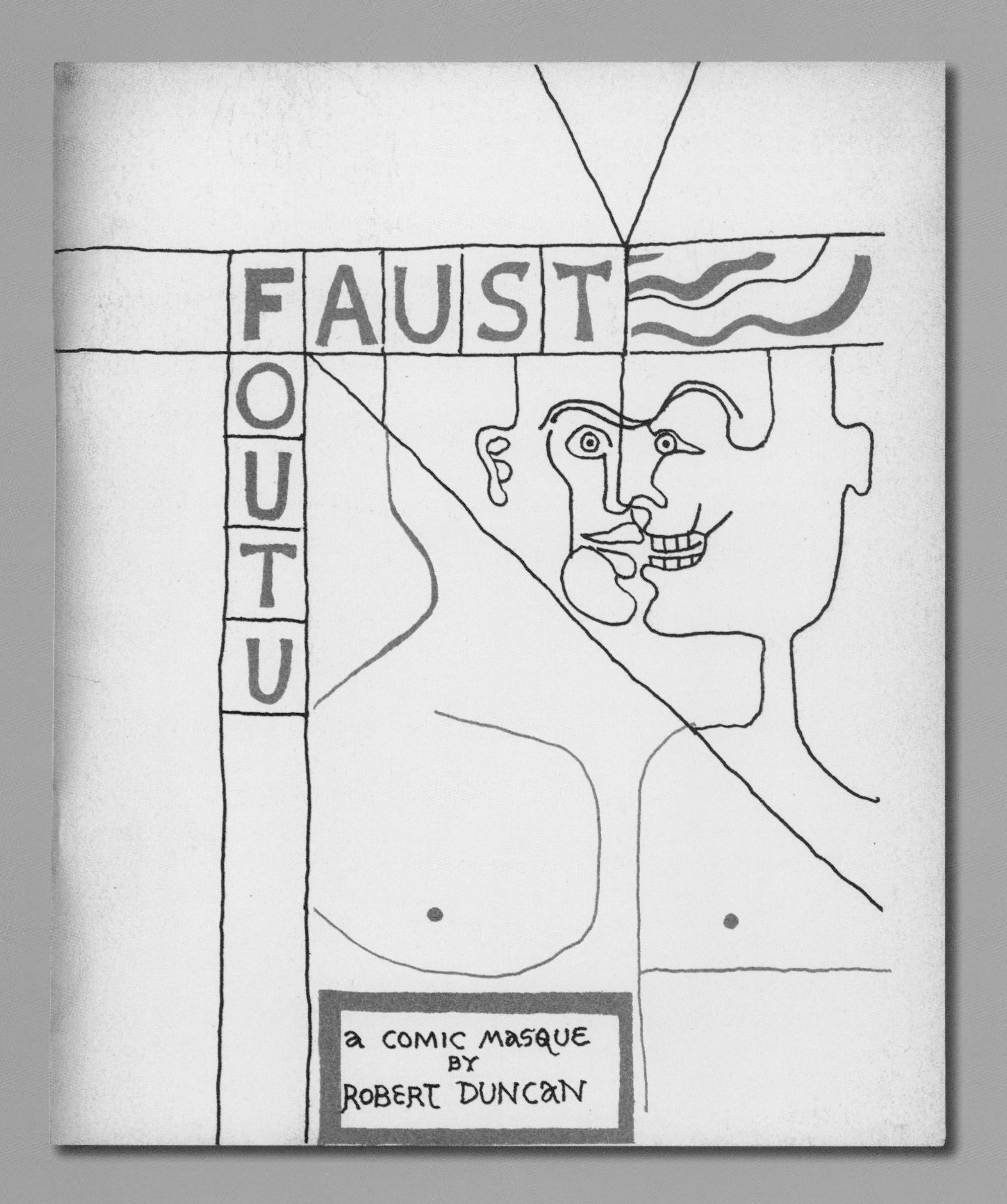

Robert Duncan
Faust Foutu
Stinson Beach, CA: Enkidu Surrogate, 1960
Illustrations by the author, limited edition of 750 copies of which 50 copies are numbered and signed, including a special color drawing by the author.
PHELAN CALIFORNIA AUTHORS COLLECTION, BOOK ARTS & SPECIAL COLLECTIONS

An Ode
and
Arcadia

Jack Spicer
Robert Duncan

Jack Spicer and Robert Duncan
An Ode and Arcadia
Berkeley: Ark Press, 1974
Printed by Wesley Tanner
GRABHORN COLLECTION ON THE HISTORY OF PRINTING, BOOK ARTS & SPECIAL COLLECTIONS

Allen Ginsberg
Wichita Vortex Sutra
[San Francisco]: Coyote;
San Francisco: Distributed by City Lights Books, 1966
PHELAN CALIFORNIA AUTHORS COLLECTION, BOOK ARTS & SPECIAL COLLECTIONS

WICHITA
VORTEX
SUTRA
ALLEN
GINSBERG

The Cockettes

The Cockettes (1969-1972) blazed like a dazzling, slightly frayed comet through the psychedelic landscape of San Francisco, creating a spectacular, subversive theater of gender pandemonium. A young New York stage actor named George Harris came to San Francisco in 1968, renamed himself Hibiscus, and in the context of communal living, drugs and revolutionary ideals, became a visionary dedicated to free art and theater, founding the Cockettes. Hibiscus took to the streets in fabulous, ceremonial hippie drag, attracting and influencing an eclectic group of gay men and straight women. Their daily life of dressing up, playacting, and sexual exploration led to the routines of a wildly transgressive theater troupe. Sylvester, one of the early members of the Cockettes, went on to have a stellar career as a chart-topping singer and performer.

Transformed by thrift-store finery and elaborate makeup, the Cockettes performed inspired midnight shows at the Palace Theater in San Francisco's North Beach neighborhood. Early productions such as *Tinsel Tarts in a Hot Coma*, and *Gone with the Showboat to Oklahoma*, were characterized by an anarchic, absurdist sensibility, non-narrative singing and dancing, and fantastically tawdry glamour. In *Pearls Over Shanghai* the Cockettes created their first all-original script, music, and lyrics. Their growing audience, decked out for the occasion, fueled the ecstatic energy. New shows were presented every few weeks and were important events for the hip and culturally adventurous.

As word about the Cockettes' shows spread to the East Coast, the group was undergoing internal difficulties—Hibiscus and several others dedicated to free theater left to form the Angels of Light, and the remaining Cockettes went to New York for a highly anticipated three-week run. Celebrities and socialites turned out in droves, but the joyously amateurish spirit of the Cockettes was lost on sophisticated New Yorkers. Returning to San Francisco, the Cockettes' unique alchemy continued long enough to produce several of their most successful shows and a lasting legacy.

The Hormel Center is fortunate to have a collection of rare Cockettes materials, donated by Kreemah Ritz, an original member of the group. Included in the collection are photographs from the production of the Cockettes' 1971 film *Trisha [Tricia] Nixon's Wedding* (other films include *Elevator Girls in Bondage* and *Luminous Procuress*), *The Cockettes Paper Doll Book*, publicity posters, and performance stills, including Kreemah Ritz as Miss Liberty.

LEFT TO RIGHT:
Fayette Hauser
Kreemah, 1970
Gelatin silver print

Concert tickets
1974 and 1979

ALL MATERIALS:
KREEMAH RITZ PAPERS

THE TRISHA NIXON WEDDING OF 1971
JUNE 12: 1971
Mr. NIXON
Pat
trisha
Ed COX
Mrs. COX
Mr. COX
Mamie
Julie NIXON
David Eisenhower
Billy Graham

$2.00
Les
Cockettes

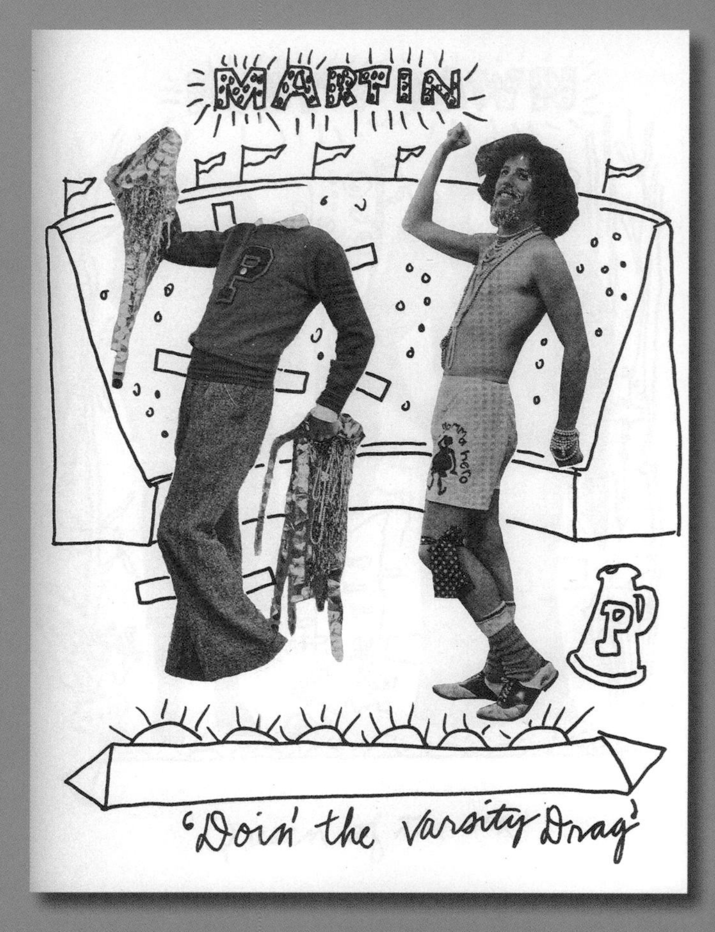
MARTIN
'Doin' the varsity Drag'

LEFT TO RIGHT, TOP TO BOTTOM:
Photographer unknown
Trisha [Tricia] Nixon Wedding
1971
Mixed media

Kreemah Ritz
Diary of a Cockette in and Around New York City
1972

Jack Flowers and Clay Geerdes
Official Cockettes Paper Doll Book
Front cover and inside pages
1971

ALL MATERIALS:
KREEMAH RITZ PAPERS

Kiki Gallery

A small gallery located in San Francisco's Mission District, the Kiki Gallery was a provocative, intelligent presence in the Bay Area art community from 1993 to 1995. Kiki's founder and director, Rick Jacobsen, shaped a lively program of exhibitions, readings, and performances by emerging artists. The confluence of innovative art, gay culture, and performance that was distinctive to Kiki had its antecedents in the mid-1950s projects of King Ubu Gallery and Six Gallery. In these pioneering artist-run spaces, Jack Spicer, Robert Duncan, Jess, Wally Hedrick, Jay De Feo, Allen Ginsberg, and others presented and supported one another's work. The same creative energies effloresced in the theatre of the Cockettes, in the conceptual art and performance movement of the 1970s, and in the rich history of alternative art spaces in the Bay Area. These energies had a brilliant, though brief, flowering at Kiki. The gallery became highly regarded for its director's imagination and fearlessness in presenting challenging new work.

In its existence of only twenty-two months, Kiki was known for many memorable shows and events, beginning with the exhibitions *Caca @ Kiki* and ending with *Piece: Nine Artists Consider Yoko Ono*. The archives includes: exhibition catalogues (*Sick Joke, Fresh Produce*), publicity materials (*Late Night with Joan Jett Blakk*), performance stills (David E. Johnston's *Gone Dollywood*), original art (Keith Mayerson's *Pinocchio the Big Fag*), and snapshots of Rick Jacobsen with Jerome Caja's work installed for the exhibition *Toilet Water*, seen in the background.

TOP TO BOTTOM:
Rebecca Jane Gleason
Gone Dollywood, c.1993
Performance piece by David E. Johnston
Pictured with Nicole Claro
Gelatin silver print

Keith Mayerson
Pinocchio the Big Fag, c.1993
Ink on vellum

ALL MATERIALS/BOTH PAGES:
KIKI GALLERY COLLECTION

LEFT TO RIGHT, TOP TO BOTTOM:
Jim Winters
***Fork Split*, c.1993**
Vinyl sticker

Maker unknown
***Fresh Produce* c.1993**
catalogue cover

Photographer unknown
Joan Jett-Blakk and Babette
c.1993
Hosts of talkshow/performance series produced by Rick Jacobsen
Gelatin silver print

Wayne Smith
***Sick Joke*, 1993**
catalogue cover

SICK JOKE

PUBLISHED ON
THE OCCASION OF

"Sick Joke"
Bitterness, Sarcasm & Irony in the Second AIDS Decade

AN EXHIBITION AT

{ KIKI }

San Francisco
Winter '93

William Moritz
John Burnside and Harry Hay
1992
Gelatin silver print
HARRY HAY PAPERS

Harry Hay

The Harry Hay papers document the life and activist legacy of Harry Hay (1912-2002)—a dynamic, visionary man considered by many to be the father of the modern gay rights movement. Hay's lifelong goal was for LGBT people to gain recognition as a cultural minority, and to be protected as such as citizens. Hay's papers are extensive, ranging from his youth as a handsome undergraduate at Stanford University to his later years as a political activist living harmoniously with his soul mate John Burnside. The papers include correspondence, photographs, and annotated research files chronicling Hay's studies of "Two-Spirit" people, music, gay culture, and leftist activism, as well as a collection of gay periodicals and newspapers. The papers document Hay's involvement with the Communist Party and his subsequent appearance before the House on Un-American Activities Committee. Hay's papers also document his part in founding the early gay rights organization, the Mattachine Society. This extensive collection was donated in 1997 by Harry Hay and John Burnside. Additional material was added up until Hay's death in 2002.

Harry Hay
Linoleum block, 1937
HARRY HAY PAPERS

A striking early linoleum block print—the block shown above—portrays Hay as a young revolutionary. At this time he was active in the Communist Party and was a member of the Hollywood Anti-Nazi League. The seeds of the Mattachine Society were planted in 1948, the year that saw the publication of Alfred Kinsey's *Sexual Behavior in the Human Male* and the birth of Hay's "International Bachelors Fraternal Order for Peace and Social Dignity." By 1951, this discussion group had transformed to the Society of Fools, then, formally, the Mattachine Society. The Mattachine Society is widely thought of as the first group of its kind for gay men, as well as the most influential. It was one of several West Coast pre-Stonewall homophile movements of the era, including liberation movements such as its lesbian counterpart, the Daughters of Bilitis. By 1952, a periodical evolved out of these discussion groups, and *ONE Magazine: The Homosexual Viewpoint* was born, along with a new corporation, ONE Inc., whose board was composed of early Mattachine members. By 1953, the original Mattachine Society dissolved, but *ONE* thrived and Hay continued to disseminate his political views. *ONE* was bold in its vision and achieved a wide circulation; by 1961, such surveys as the "Homosexual Bill of Rights" were being distributed—strong statements urging gays to consider the personal in relation to the political.

In the 1960s, Hay met and began his lifelong relationship with John Burnside, who helped found the Circle of Loving Companions, a group that espoused Hay's belief that gay people make separate and unique contributions. The Circle of Loving Companions was one of many groups comprising the growing gay liberation movement. At this time, Hay was active in the anti-Vietnam War movement and especially the antidraft movement, helping distribute information to gays and lesbians, who, Hay believed, had different counseling needs.

Photographer unknown
Harry Hay appearing before HUAC, 1955
Gelatin silver print
HARRY HAY PAPERS

RIGHT:
Citizens Committee to Preserve American Freedoms
c.1955
Courage is Contagious: The Bill of Rights versus The Un-American Activities Committee
HARRY HAY PAPERS

Jim Gruber
First Mattachine Society gathering, Christmas 1951
Pictured: Harry Hay (sitting) then left to right on floor: Dale Jennings, Rudi Gernreich, Stan Witt, Bob Hull, Chuck Rowland (with glasses), and Paul Bernard
Gelatin silver print
HARRY HAY PAPERS

COURAGE IS CONTAGIOUS

The Bill of Rights

versus

The Un-American Activities Committee

Fifteen Cents

Photographer unknown
Harry Hay protesting Dan White's parole, 1984
Gelatin silver print
HARRY HAY PAPERS

By the 1970s, Hay's focus on gays and lesbians as "a separate people with unique contributions to make to the straight world" had found a collective, communal outlet. Hay and Burnside had been living in New Mexico, and had become involved with such causes as the Gay American Indian Movement, as well as the local gay rights group, the Lambdas of Santa Fe. It was here that Hay conducted research on Native American "Two-Spirit" people—shamans considered to be both man and woman.

The 1970s saw a rise in gay subcultures, and two striking figures dominated this period: the Clone—a hyper-macho, masculinist, and homogeneous gay male type; and the Faerie—a gay man who embraced gender differences and blurred gender stereotypes. In 1979, the first "Spiritual Conference for Radical Faeries" was held—the name coined by Hay from the word "radical," meaning "root" and "politically/culturally extreme," and the word "faerie," which alluded to the pejorative connotation of effeminate masculinity but also to magical spirits, furthering the view of gay people as coming from a separate tribe. The Radical Faeries, while creating a sacred space for spirituality and espousing an anti-assimilationist form of gay liberation, also produced art and published numerous periodicals such as *RFD*, *Raddish*, *Salt & Sage*, and the *Fifth Element*. Faerie gatherings and groups spread across the nation—communal land was purchased, and the Faeries proved themselves more than just a back-to-nature collective. The archives contains several photo albums depicting their elaborate rituals and communal sexuality.

Throughout the 1980s, Hay's activism continued in the struggle against AIDS, as well as in events such as the "Keep Dan White Out of L.A." protest. During the 1990s, Hay worked tirelessly to disseminate his views that gays should reject heterosexual models. Hay believed in casting off the "green frog skin" of hetero-imitation to reveal the faerie within. His death in 2002 ended an extraordinary life, and almost a century of activism.

The Vanguard
Issues from 1966
San Francisco
HARRY HAY PAPERS

Periodicals

The Hormel Center contains a collection of historical and contemporary periodicals created by, for, and about LGBT communities across the United States and abroad. Interfiled within the library's Magazines and Newspapers Center, these periodicals are an invaluable record of the development of LGBT identity, community, and culture, and they have played a critical role in political activism. Reading through the archives' periodical collection, one witnesses the evolution of LGBT discourse and creative expression from its beginnings in typed and mimeographed artists' books and newsletters—akin to Russian Samizdat—to more contemporary magazines that look and feel mainstream by comparison.

Many of the earlier periodicals in the Hormel collection, dating from approximately 1947 to 1975, were self-published and short-lived, issued irregularly and distributed unsystematically. Though such conditions make it challenging to acquire and preserve these early materials, the diligent collecting efforts of librarians, small-press publishers, and gay and lesbian authors have resulted in substantial donations of material to the Hormel Center. Not infrequently, important periodicals have entered the archives without fanfare, tucked within personal papers and other ephemera. For example, photocopies of the groundbreaking lesbian periodical *Vice Versa*, first published in 1947, were included in the wealth of material donated by Barbara Grier and Donna McBride.

DER EIGENE

LEFT:
Adolf Brand
Der Eigene, 1906
First gay journal

RIGHT:
"Lisa Ben"
Vice Versa
Multiple issues, 1947-1948
Carbon paper, mimeograph
BARBARA GRIER AND DONNA MCBRIDE/NAIAD PRESS COLLECTION

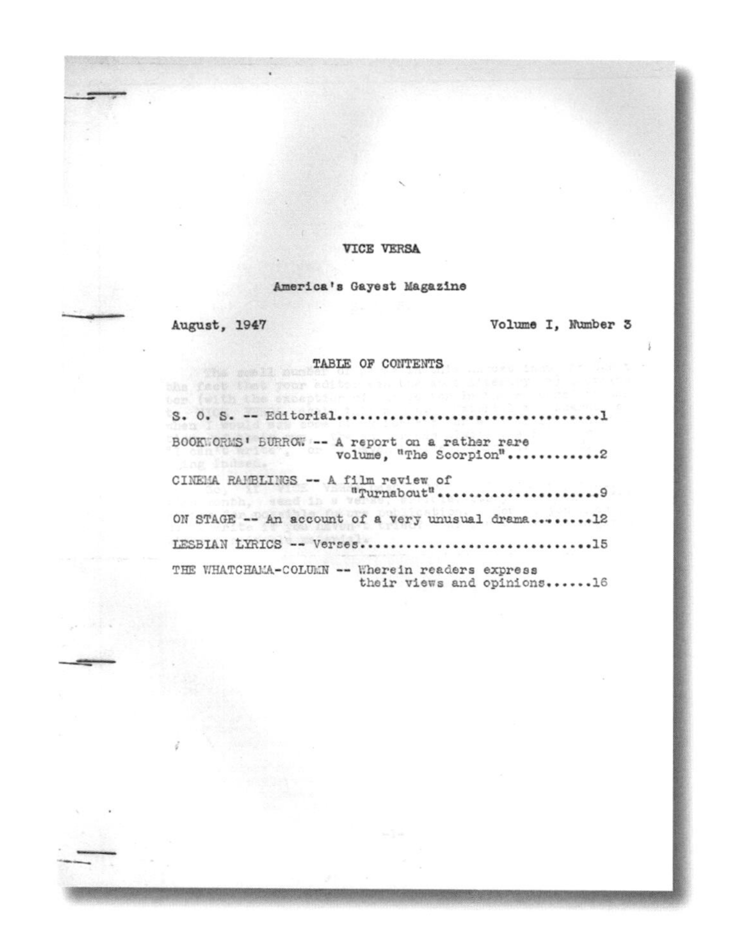

VICE VERSA

America's Gayest Magazine

August, 1947 Volume I, Number 3

TABLE OF CONTENTS

Considered the world's first gay periodical, *Der Eigene* ("The Self-Owners"), began as a German anarchist journal. Published by Adolf Brand from 1896 to 1931, *Der Eigene* became the voice of a small movement that advocated Classical Greek pederasty—highly ritualized sexual relationships between men and boys—as a cure for what some saw as the alarming effeminacy of German culture. The Hormel Center archives contain Volume Six of *Der Eigene*, which includes some of the earliest material on gay life in San Francisco. The views expressed in *Der Eigene* contrasted sharply with those of another Berlin group, the Scientific Humanitarian Committee. Founded by Dr. Magnus Hirschfeld in Berlin in 1897, the Scientific Humanitarian Committee was the world's first gay rights organization. The committee supported feminism, liberal democracy, and egalitarian relationships between consenting adults. In 1919, Hirschfeld opened the Institute for Sexual Science in Berlin. Its library contained one of Europe's most important collections of material on human sexuality. In 1933, the Nazis raided the institute, burning Hirschfeld's library in a huge nighttime bonfire. Hirschfeld escaped the Nazis but died two years later in exile in France.

Vice Versa, subtitled "America's Gayest Magazine," is the first known lesbian publication in the United States. From 1947-48, nine editions of ten copies each were authored, edited, typed, and hand-distributed by Lisa Ben, a pseudonym used by the author. *Vice Versa* was a labor of love and is considered the radical ancestor of contemporary gay journals. The author named the publication *Vice Versa* to call attention to the fact that being gay or lesbian is not a "vice," but rather the "versa," or opposite of, vice. The author typed *Vice Versa* five carbon copies at a time from her office at RKO Studios. *Vice Versa* was distributed without charge, primarily in lesbian bars, where, in turn, readers passed it on to others. In this manner, *Vice Versa* was read by hundreds of people before it nearly disappeared.

Readers of contemporary queer publications may not be aware of the personal and professional hardship experienced by early gay and lesbian publishers and authors. Contained within the Hormel Center's archives are many cautionary tales about individual freedom and personal expression. One astonishing example is the story of *ONE* Magazine.

one
APRIL 1965
FIFTY CENTS

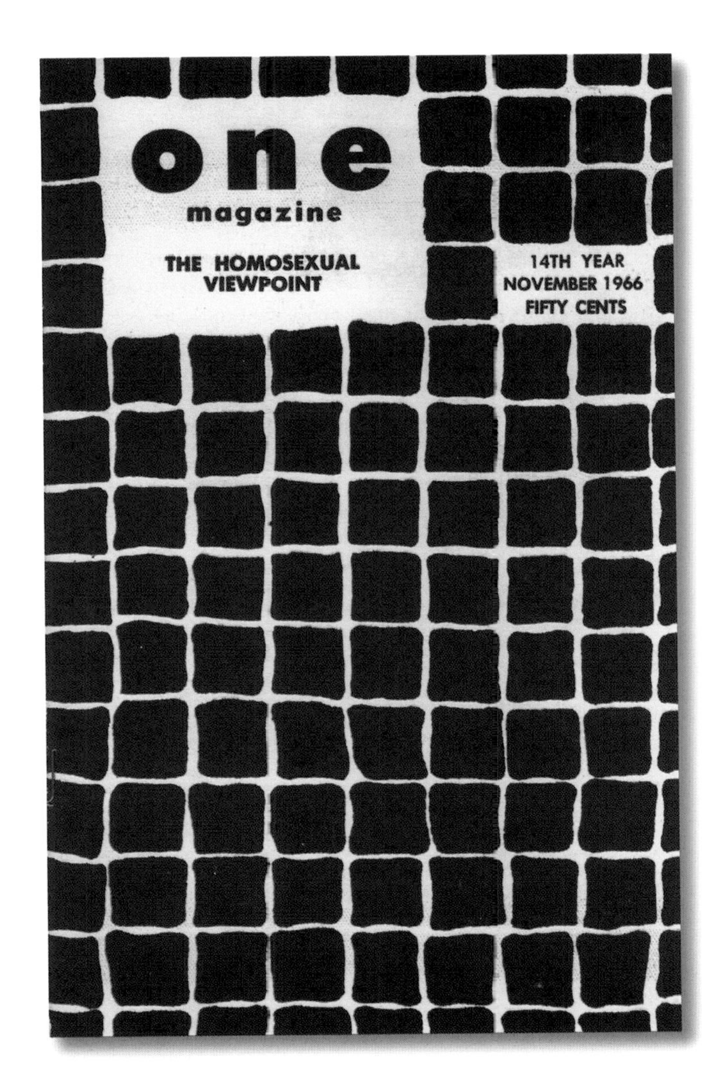

ONE
Los Angeles, 1953-68
Various issues
HARRY HAY PAPERS

ONE Magazine was founded by Harry Hay and a group of Mattachine Society members in Los Angeles, California, in 1952. It was produced monthly from 1953 to 1968. *ONE* was published by ONE Inc., an offshoot of the Mattachine Society, one of the earliest gay-liberation organizations in America. The magazine's name derives from a quote by nineteenth-century British essayist Thomas Carlyle: "A mystical bond of brotherhood makes all men one." In 1953 and again in 1954, *ONE Magazine* was nearly shut down when the U.S. postmaster of Los Angeles deemed its content obscene and seized all extant copies. *ONE's* publishers brought a legal suit against the agency, and the ensuing publicity in the Los Angeles Times, the New York Times, and the Washington Post brought unprecedented national attention to gay rights issues.

ONE's case was resolved in 1958, when the United States Supreme Court reversed a ruling by a federal district court judge and cleared the way for national postal distribution of the periodical. In an opinion by Justice John Marshall Harlan, the Supreme Court ruled that the postal service could not presume that gay-oriented materials were pornographic, opening up the distribution of sexually frank homoerotic magazines and newspapers. It was a landmark ruling in achieving protection for erotic materials that diverged from the heterosexual norm.

The Personal into the Political

The phrase "the personal is political" was first employed in the women's rights movement. Over time the meaning broadened to include the concept that personal choice directly affects political systems and social structures. Some people's life choices require that they diverge from social norms, shifting their personal and professional lives into the political sphere. An outstanding example of LGBT forthrightness is contained in the "coming out" letter that Republican party strategist and fundraiser Marvin Liebman published in the politically conservative *National Review*. He later wrote the book *Coming Out Conservative*, which describes his life as a gay man. The creation of untraditional families is one example of social politics at work; by pursuing life on their own terms, such families are engaged in a form of activism. In the groundbreaking documentary *Word Is Out*, Peter Adair interviewed members of the LGBT community; his artistic editing highlighted the commonalities between their experiences.

Throughout history, LGBT people have questioned social roles, recognizing that their experience does not mirror that of the status quo or the majority. Deeply committed to personal and social change, they made difficult decisions, often in isolation, to make a difference in their communities. William Billings, arrested and imprisoned in 1954 for "indecent acts," fought for his civil rights, ultimately obtaining a pardon from the governor of Colorado. Magnus Hirschfeld's pioneering work in the early part of the twentieth century sought to educate scientists and legal officials on the complexities of human sexuality. Like Harry Hay and others who later contributed to shaping modern gay identity, Magnus Hirschfeld was drawn to the cultural experience of indigenous people—cultures that traditionally celebrate rather than pathologize diverse ways of being.

Magnus Hirschfeld, founder of the Institute for Sexual Science, was a leader in the study of sexuality in Berlin in the 1920s and 1930s. Along with the Scientific-Humanitarian Committee, cofounded by Hirschfeld in 1897, Hirschfeld worked to remove Paragraph 175—the portion that forbade sex between men—from German law. Ultimately their efforts were unsuccessful. In contrast to the egalitarian and liberal ideology of the Scientific-Humanitarian Committee, the journal *Der Eigene*, which began in 1896, advocated a more patriarchal and conservative approach, even though it also emphasized same-sex relationships. With the rise of the Nazi party, Hirschfeld, an openly homosexual Jew, was forced to flee Germany. The events of that time are the subject of Rob Epstein's film *Paragraph 175*. In light of Hirschfeld's life and exile, the artist Cathy Cade's documentary photographs are especially evocative. So, too, is William Billings's scrapbook documenting his incarceration for being gay. The way in which Billings assembled his obsessive and revealing visual journals is an inspirational, intricate collage.

Cathy Cade
Commie, Faggot, Queer and Proud
1977
Gelatin silver print
CATHY CADE PHOTOGRAPHS
COLLECTION

The 1930s El Dorado tokens, which historians believe were meant to be exchanged for a dance with a transvestite in the Weimar-era club, are a lasting reminder of a liberal and liberating era. Daniel Nicoletta's photograph of the dressing room at Finocchio's on its last night of business documents a significant event in San Francisco's LGBT history and presents a poignant counterpoint to the tokens.

The lives of LGBT people often take unexpected turns leading to more public arenas. Harvey Milk was one such man—a gay small business owner (Milk owned a camera shop in San Francisco's Castro neighborhood) who changed the nation's political landscape by holding civic office as an openly gay man. Milk saw politics as the most efficient means of fighting bigotry and enacting the social changes that he and many others saw necessary. And like others before him, Harvey Milk understood the risk that he was taking by being open and out.

In the 1980s the advent of AIDS required a new level of political activism and awareness, and in the midst of a catastrophic health crisis, an extraordinary collective response unfolded. Organizations such as ACT UP (the AIDS Coalition to Unleash Power), Queer Nation, and OutRage! shared a commitment to direct action—speaking out against the homophobia pervasive in our communities, government, the health system, schools, and the media. The great energy, creativity, and political vision of dedicated grassroots activists found expression in the bold graphics and powerful language of the posters, stickers, fliers and newsletters that were produced and distributed in New York, San Francisco, and many other cities worldwide.

AIDS and its devastating personal and communal effects are the subjects of Rob Epstein and Jeffrey Friedman's *Common Threads* and Randy Shilts's *And the Band Played On*. The material from Ward 86 (later Ward 5B/5A) documents activity at San Francisco General Hospital's AIDS ward—on the cutting edge of AIDS treatment in the nation. Collected by the nurses as well as patients and family members, the Ward 5B/5A material complements many of the other items in the archives by detailing institutional concerns and practices as well as personal narratives and community responses. The archives contain photographs that reveal the reality of AIDS within the personal and private realms of hospitals. One such photograph by Rick Gerharter depicts Rita Rocket, who initiated a weekly brunch for AIDS patients and their friends and families. Such photographs make a connection between the isolation of illness and the impact of HIV/AIDS on the broader community. Amongst the papers of J. Allen Carson, a member of San Francsco's ACT UP, Queer Nation, and OutRage!, are many examples of the brilliant graphic materials created by activist organizations in the 1980s and early 1990s, which speak to the passionate and dedicated efforts of the LGBT community in the fight against all forms of discrimination.

The debate over the appropriateness of gays in the military has raged for decades—with many courageous men and women coming out in the armed forces, refusing to hide their identity because of their country's small-mindedness. And most recently, the movement to legalize gay marriage has both intensified and expanded, bringing this fundamental civil rights issue to the forefront of the nation's consciousness. All of these stories demonstrate individuals redefining their relationship to society, risking their lives to change the world.

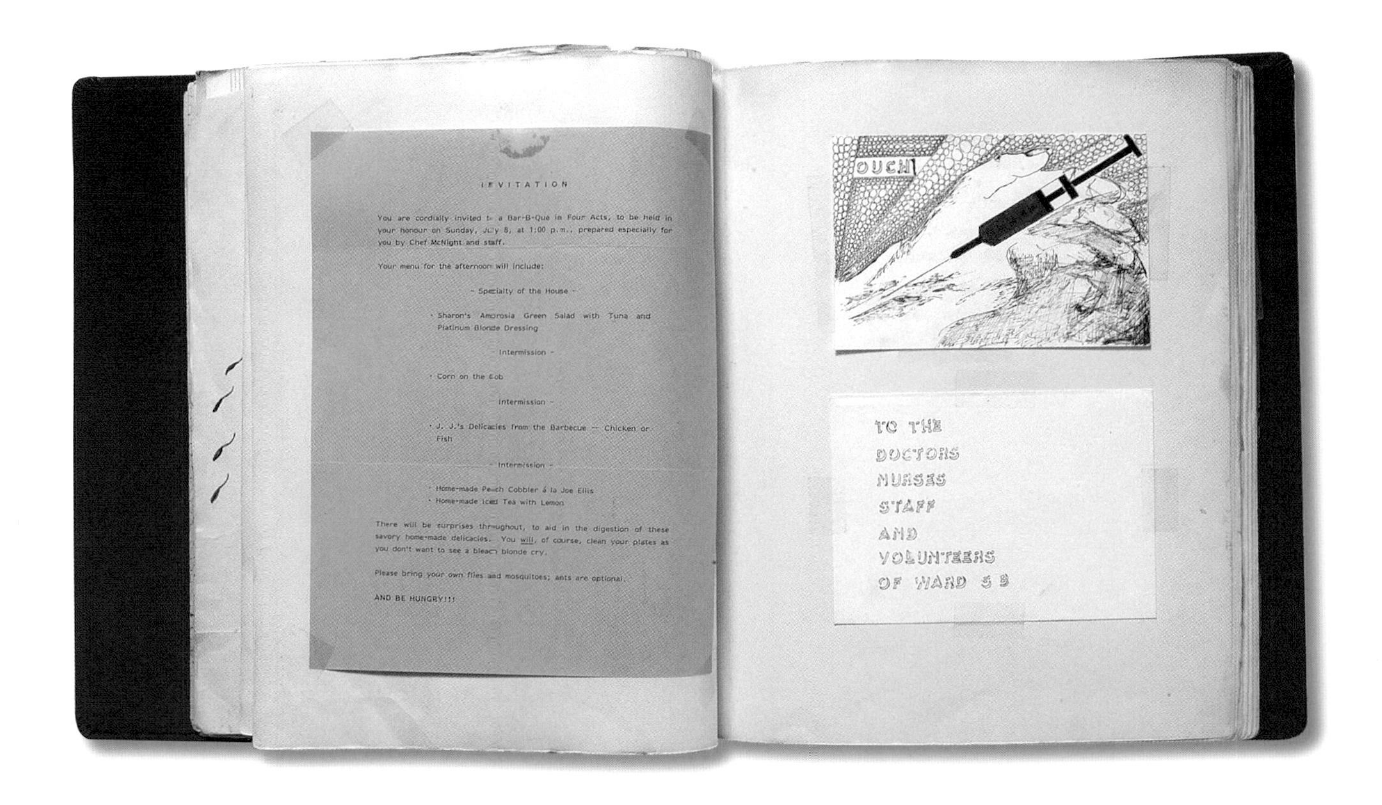

INVITATION

You are cordially invited to a Bar-B-Que in Four Acts, to be held in your honour on Sunday, July 8, at 1:00 p.m., prepared especially for you by Chef McNight and staff.

Your menu for the afternoon will include:

- Specialty of the House -

· Sharon's Amorosia Green Salad with Tuna and Platinum Blonde Dressing

- Intermission -

· Corn on the Cob

- Intermission -

· J. J.'s Delicacies from the Barbecue -- Chicken or Fish

- Intermission -

· Home-made Peach Cobbler á la Joe Ellis
· Home-made Iced Tea with Lemon

There will be surprises throughout, to aid in the digestion of these savory home-made delicacies. You will, of course, clean your plates as you don't want to see a bleach blonde cry.

Please bring your own flies and mosquitoes; ants are optional.

AND BE HUNGRY!!!

OFFICE OF THE MAYOR
SAN FRANCISCO

DIANNE FEINSTEIN

September 27, 1984

Staff at Ward 5B
San Francisco General Hospital
1001 Potrero Avenue
San Francisco, California 94110

Dear Staff at Ward 5B:

I have received your September 21 letter regarding expansion of inpatient services for AIDS patients at San Francisco General Hospital.

Please be assured that I am aware and concerned about the needs of AIDS patients at San Francisco General and elsewhere. I will be reviewing the Department's plans to cope with anticipated future patients. I very much appreciate your concern for your patients and your dedication to your jobs.

Sincerely yours,

Dianne Feinstein
Mayor

DF/MK:la

cc: Dr. Mervyn Silverman, Director of Health

San Francisco General Hospital
AIDS Ward Archives
Scrapbook, Vol. 1, 1983
SAN FRANCISCO HISTORY CENTER

El Dorado Medallions, Berlin
c.1930
Metal dance tokens
(shown front and back)

RIGHT:
ACT UP San Francisco
***Stickers*, c.1990**

DYKE POWER

FAG POWER

DYKES TAKE OVER THE WORLD

DYKE POWER

FAG POWER

DYKES TAKE OVER THE WORLD

DYKE POWER

FAG POWER

DYKES TAKE OVER THE WORLD

DYKE POWER

FAG POWER

DYKES TAKE OVER THE WORLD

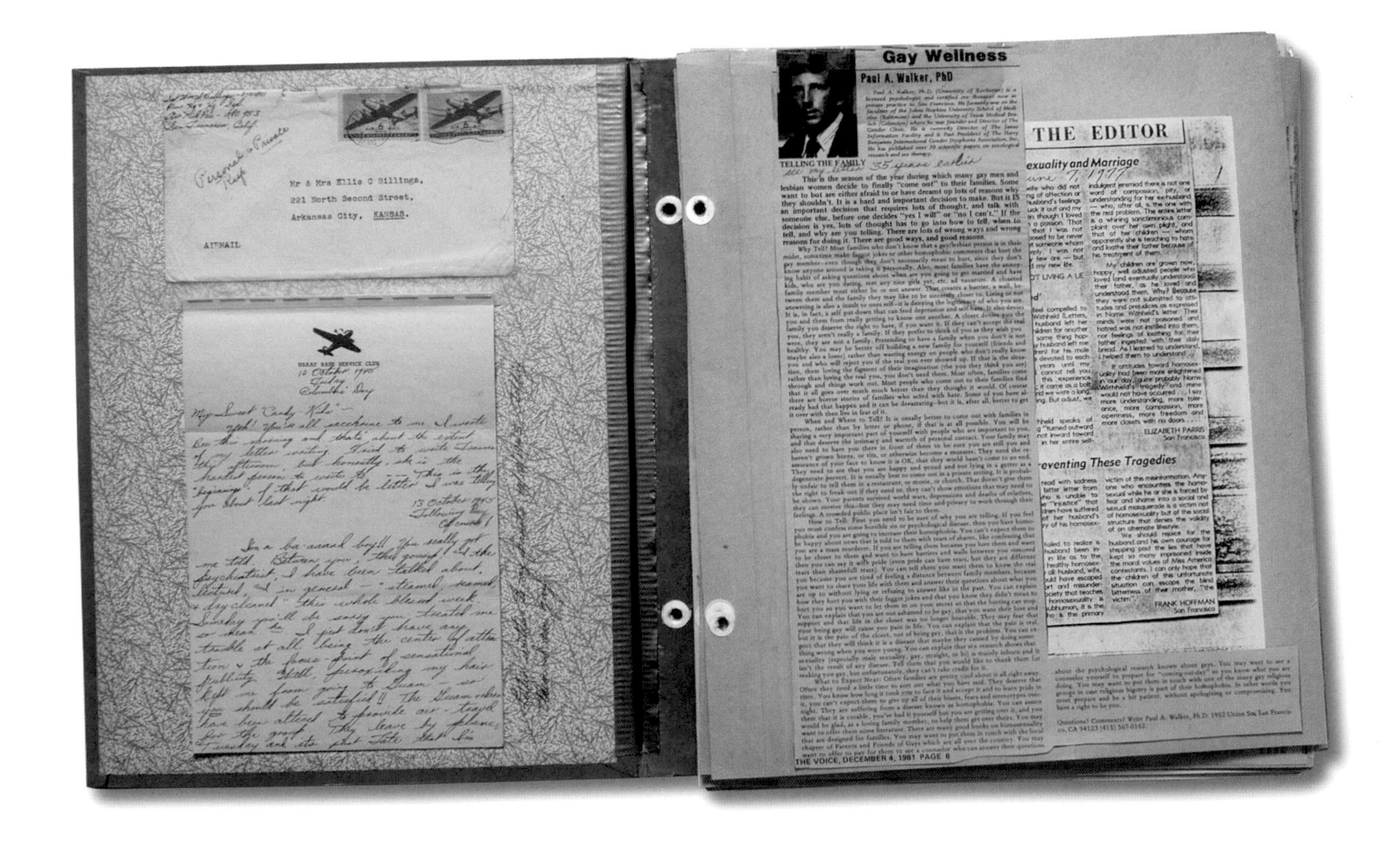

William Billings

William Wilmer Billings was a schoolteacher, a founding member of the Council on Religion and the Homosexual, and a candidate for San Francisco supervisor who ran against Dan White. Billings donated a small but critical collection of materials to the Hormel Center in 1994, the most notable items being two scrapbooks that chronicle his life with devotion and honesty. The first scrapbook includes all of the material relating to Billings's arrest in 1954 for "unnatural carnal copulation," his subsequent imprisonment, parole, and, finally, his unconditional pardon from the governor of Colorado in October 1966. It took over ten years and four governors before Billings's pardon was granted. Billings's scrapbook reveals the heartbreaking story of a man persecuted for his personal life.

The second scrapbook, entitled "Gay Scrapbook," begins with his 1945 handwritten "coming out" letter to his parents, and continues with newspaper articles, magazine clippings, invitations, pamphlets, and correspondence from various friends up to 1994. The subjects in this scrapbook include gay marriage, gay athletes, homosexuality as a product of genetics or upbringing, openly gay politicians, gays in the military, gay parenting, parents of gays, gays and religion, and AIDS, among many others. Many of the subjects that Billings chronicled in his notebooks in the 1970s, such as same-sex marriage, are now emerging again as critical issues.

William Billings
Gay Scrapbook
1945–1994
WILLIAM BILLINGS
PAPERS

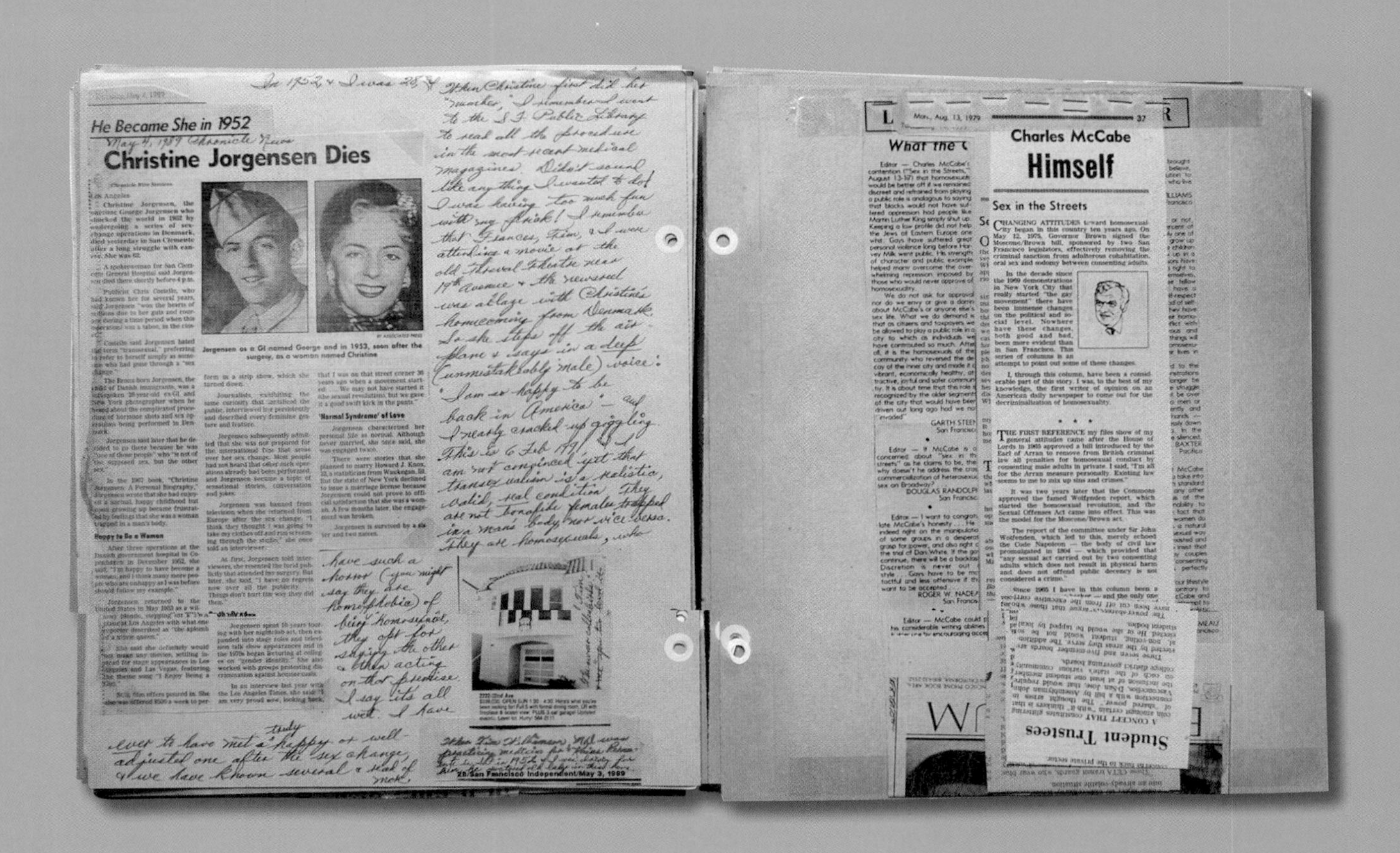
He Became She in 1952
Christine Jorgensen Dies
Charles McCabe
Himself
Sex in the Streets
Student Trustees

TO WHOM IT MAY CONCERN:
John L. Burton
Mr. William Billings
790 Post Street, Apt. 60
San Francisco, California
It's Official
Gays Are Sane
GAYS
SENATE
CALIFORNIA LEGISLATURE
William W. Billings
790 Post Street, Apt. 60
San Francisco, California 94109

LOWENTHAL & LOWENTHAL
and
RONALD D. RATTNER
405 Montgomery Street
San Francisco, California 94104
Telephone: 986-5388
Attorneys for Plaintiffs

IN THE UNITED STATES DISTRICT COURT

FOR THE NORTHERN DISTRICT OF CALIFORNIA

SOUTHERN DIVISION

EVANDER C. SMITH; HERBERT DONALDSON; ELLIOTT LEIGHTON; NANCY MAY; and THE COUNCIL ON RELIGION AND THE HOMO-SEXUAL, INC., a California non-profit corporation, on behalf of itself and its officers, members and affiliates,

Plaintiffs,

v.

THOMAS J. CAHILL; JOHN A. ENGLER; WILLISON H. LINGAFELTER; JOHN CASSIDY; RUDOLPH NIETO; RICHARD CASTRO; JACK E. TOOMEY; MICHAEL BRUSH; TED LUSHER; HOWARD WHITMAN; JAMES HIGGINS; MARGARET HARTMAN; WILLIAM ROBERTS; FRANK MOSER; WAYNE CLEMENT; J. TAYLOR; D. J. SULLIVAN; FRED WILSON; ROBERT SMITH; DAROL SMITH; FIRST DOE to SEVENTH-FIFTH DOE, inclusive, and THE CITY AND COUNTY OF SAN FRANCISCO, a California municipal corporation,

Defendants.

NO. 44390

COMPLAINT FOR DEPRIVATIONS OF CIVIL LIBERTIES

FIRST CLAIM

I

This action arises under 42 U.S.C. § 1983, § 1985 and § 1988. The Court has jurisdiction under 28 U.S.C. § 1343 and § 1331, and under its pendent jurisdiction.

Evander Smith

Evander Smith's California Hall files document the watershed moment that united San Francisco's homophile organizations into an active political force. This event was the San Francisco equivalent of New York's Stonewall riots and it happened on January 1, 1965, four years before Stonewall.

Smith was a lawyer retained by the Council on Religion and the Homosexual, a group formed in 1964 in the San Francisco area to establish a dialogue between a number of progressive Protestant religious organizations and gays and lesbians who felt abandoned by the religious establishment. The founding members included representatives from all of the homophile organizations in the city and representatives from several Protestant churches.

As a fundraiser for the new organization, a Mardi Gras-themed ball was scheduled to take place on New Year's Day, 1965, at the California Hall. This was a private event, open to ticket holders only, and the organizers met with the San Francisco Police Department to ensure that things would go smoothly. On the day of the event, however, a large number of police appeared at the hall with klieg lights and a photographer, recording the faces of everyone who entered the building. The police requested entry to inspect the group's permits—a standard practice at events where liquor was available. The officers then left the building, returning later with another request for entry. This time their request was denied due to their lack of a search warrant. It was at this point that lawyers Evander Smith, Herbert Donaldson, and Elliot Leighton, as well as ticket-taker Nancy May, were arrested.

At the ball, the ministers and their wives were firsthand witnesses to the type of unfair treatment regularly experienced by gays and lesbians. "ANGRY MINISTERS RIP POLICE" reads a January 3, 1965, headline in the *San Francisco Chronicle*. The article continues: "Ministers of four Protestant denominations accused the Police Department yesterday of 'intimidation, broken promises and obvious hostility' in breaking up a private benefit for homosexuals at California Hall Friday night." The community's indignation was expressed in many letters to the *Chronicle's* editor. On February 12, 1965, the *Chronicle* reported that the judge halted the trial on a technicality and directed the jury to return a verdict of not guilty against the lawyers. The suit against Smith, Donaldson, Leighton, and May was dismissed. They, in turn, sued the city and finally won in 1974.

Evander Smith
Trial papers, documents
c.1965
EVANDER SMITH PAPERS

LEFT TO RIGHT:
Daniel Nicoletta
The Empress Coronation
Former Empress José Sarria, Harvey
Milk and Mavis, presenting an
anonymous donation for the purchase
of uniforms for the 1st Gay and Lesbian
***Freedom Marching Band*, 1978**
Gelatin silver print
DANIEL NICOLETTA
PHOTOGRAPHS COLLECTION

Harvey Milk
***Appointment book*, 1978**
HARVEY MILK ARCHIVES–
SCOTT SMITH COLLECTION

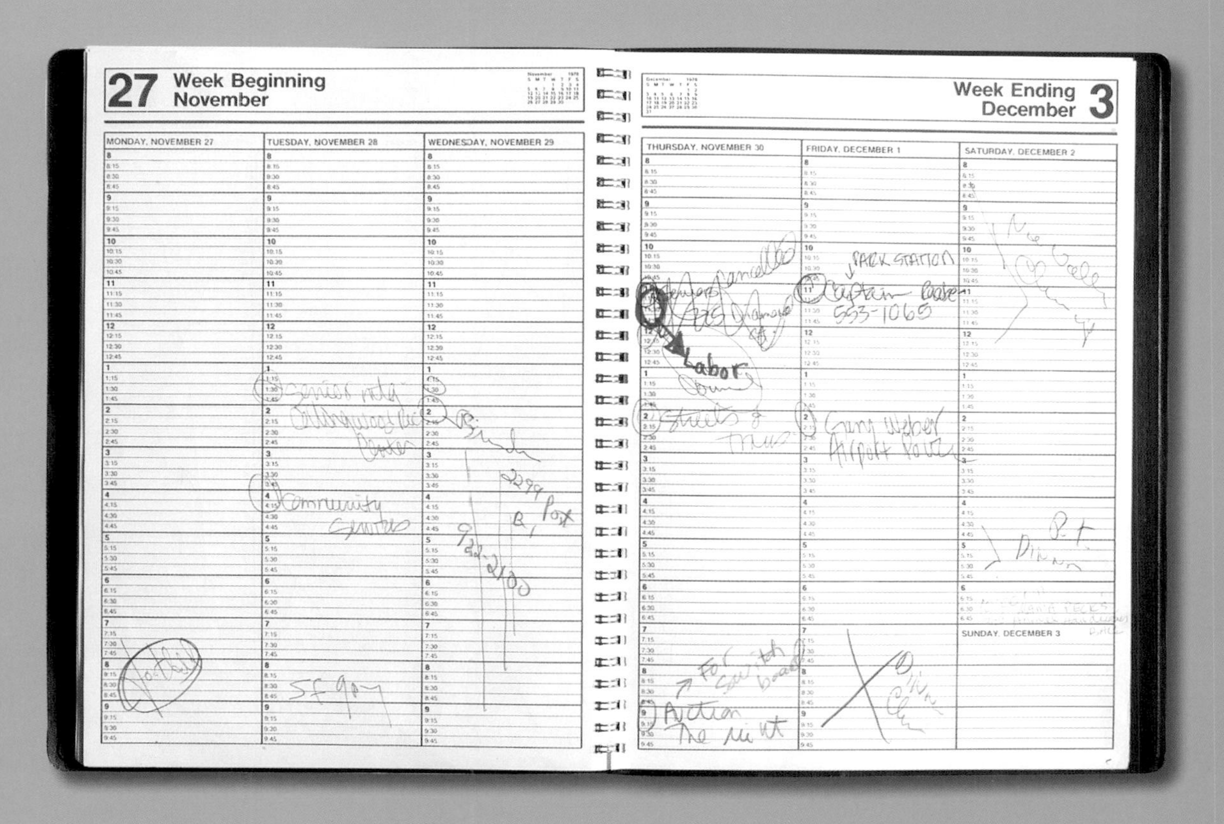

Harvey Milk

Harvey Milk was a gay rights activist, and the first openly gay man elected to the San Francisco Board of Supervisors. Randy Shilts's biography *The Mayor of Castro Street* and Rob Epstein's film *The Times of Harvey Milk* document Milk's political rise within the context of the development of the LGBT community. Like Harry Hay and Barbara Grier, Harvey Milk was an individual whose personal life shaped his professional career. His drive to represent a group of people who had been silenced and ignored made him a figure of national and international standing. Milk became a visible symbol of the LGBT community's emergence as a political force. It is no wonder, then, that the grief caused by the assassinations of Harvey Milk and Mayor George Moscone by Dan White unified the LGBT community as never before. The lenient sentence that White received for the double murder resulted in a riot at San Francisco City Hall. Daniel Nicoletta's photographs of the White Night riots powerfully capture the sheer force of the community's outrage.

Elva Smith, mother of Milk's partner Scott Smith, donated the Harvey Milk Archives/Scott Smith Collection to the Hormel Center in 1996. The collection contains the personal and political papers of Milk, the personal papers of Scott Smith, and the collection of the Harvey Milk Archives and the Harvey Milk Estate. Milk's political papers include hand-edited drafts of his speeches, such as his famous 1977 speech "You've Got to Give 'em Hope," and his writings, office files, appointment books, and related ephemera from his campaigns.

MOSCONE, MILK SHOT TO DEATH

Gunfire at City Hall — Ex-supervisor White held

Stocks up 3.72 Page 58

San Francisco Examiner

★★★★ EXTRA Complete stocks

114th Year No. 145 Monday, November 27, 1978 20¢

Aide: White 'a wild man'

LEFT TO RIGHT, TOP TO BOTTOM:
Daniel Nicoletta
White Night Riot, May 21, 1979
Gelatin silver print
DANIEL NICOLETTA
PHOTOGRAPHS COLLECTION

Daniel Nicoletta
Harvey Milk's Suit (Self portrait in the suit Harvey Milk was wearing the day he was assassinated)
A meditation on all anti-queer violence
1995
Gelatin silver print
DANIEL NICOLETTA
PHOTOGRAPHS COLLECTION

San Francisco Examiner, 1978
Headline announcing Harvey Milk's assassination
HARVEY MILK ARCHIVES–
SCOTT SMITH COLLECTION

Gary Fisher
Notebook 8 (detail)
1993
GARY FISHER PAPERS

Personal Chronicles

A man kept a diary for ten years, creating a narrative of his life in San Francisco's gay community. In his will, Vincent bequeathed them to Elizabeth Stone who had been his high school English teacher a quarter century earlier. Enclosed within the box of diaries was a letter which began "Dear Elizabeth, You must be wondering why I left you my diaries in my will. After all, we have not seen each other in over twenty years . . ."

Through the diaries, Stone learned of Vincent's daily life, travels, loves, friendships, and his devastating death from AIDS in 1995—and came to know the man her former student had become. As his story unfolded, she responded with a spectrum of emotions—judgment, anger, affection, grief, and compassion. She became aware of the impact that she had made in his life, and was challenged by the diaries to reflect upon her own life and mortality. Vincent's voice, his presence, came alive for her, and the roles of teacher and student underwent a profound shift.

Elizabeth Stone was moved to write about this revelatory and transformative experience. Her book *A Boy I Once Knew: What a Teacher Learned from Her Student* was published in 2002. She subsequently donated to the Hormel Center archives the box of Vincent's diaries that had so unexpectedly changed her life.

The Gary Fisher papers include manuscripts, diaries, correspondence, and publications. They were donated to the center by Eve Kosossky Sedgwick. Fisher began keeping journals in high school and continued the practice until his death from AIDS at 32. In a distinctly honest, witty, compassionate voice, he detailed his experiences as a gay African American man, a writer, and a person living with AIDS. The diaries are vibrant with his poetry and richly colored drawings, and reflective of his passionate engagement with the intertwining dimensions of sexuality, race, the body, life, and death.

Writer, activist, and academic Jewelle Gomez, who serves on the Hormel Endowment Committee, has donated a collection of her personal papers to the archives. Within the collection is a box of private journals containing fragments of poetry, memories, and musings interspersed with reflections on daily life. The author of seven books, Gomez's work also appears in various periodicals and anthologies, and ranges from fiction to personal and political essays, poetry, and criticism. The journals offer rare insights into the experiences that have shaped her life and work.

TOP TO BOTTOM:
Jewelle Gomez
Journals
c. 1976
JEWELLE GOMEZ
COLLECTION

Vincent
Diaries and ephemera
c.1984–1995
VINCENT DIARIES
COLLECTION

Ann P. Meredith
Dr. Tom Waddell, founder of the Gay Games, and Jessica Lewinstein-Waddell, daughter of Dr. Waddell and Sara Lewinstein, San Francisco Gay Games, Triumph in '86, 1986
Gelatin silver print
ANN P. MEREDITH PHOTOGRAPHS COLLECTION

Gay Games

Any discussion of the Gay Games movement must begin with Dr. Tom Waddell. A physician, lifelong athlete, and sports enthusiast, Waddell finished in sixth place in the decathlon at the 1968 Olympics in Mexico City. Recognizing the importance that sports played in his own sense of self-esteem and discipline, he envisioned an arena to promote sports and positive self-image within what was then a largely bar- and club-centered community. The hallmark of the games that Waddell envisioned would be participation and inclusion regardless of sexual orientation or age. In 1980 Waddell formed the United States Gay Olympics Committee with Mark Brown and Paul Mart. The committee would later become San Francisco Arts and Athletics, and much later, the Federation of Gay Games.

1982 GAY OLYMPIC GAMES
AUGUST 28-SEPTEMBER 5 · KEZAR STADIUM · SAN FRANCISCO
1982 GAY GAMES
AUGUST 28-SEPTEMBER 5 · KEZAR STADIUM · SAN FRANCISCO

LEFT TO RIGHT, TOP TO BOTTOM:
Maker unknown
Two posters with and without the word "Olympic," 1982

Maker unknown
"Sports Director" jacket and black bowling jacket with political pins & buttons, c.1982

Maker unknown
Gay Games Medals
1982 and 1986

ALL MATERIALS:
FEDERATION OF GAY GAMES RECORDS

Perhaps the best-known story connected with the games is that of the legal proceedings with the U.S. Olympic Committee over the Gay Games' use of the word "Olympic." Using the Olympic Games as a model and in keeping with other events such as the Special Olympics, Waddell had conceived of the "Gay Olympic Games" and publicized it as such. Nineteen days prior to the event, the USOC obtained an injunction forbidding the use of the word "Olympic" in any of the event's materials. Of course, by that time press packets, T-shirts, and posters had already been printed. One can see the evidence of this last-minute name change in the posters and T-shirts produced for the games—some with the words "Gay Olympic Games" and the other with the word "Olympic" blocked out. It was thus that the "Gay Games" were born.

The success of the 1982 Gay Games in San Francisco spawned a movement that continues to this day. The federation oversees the organization of the quadrennial event, which has taken place in San Francisco (1986), Vancouver (1990), New York City (1994), Amsterdam (1998), and Sydney (2002). In addition to the games, there are now gay and lesbian sports groups in many cities around the world that meet to bowl, run, bike, swim, row, and play softball, to name just a few of the sports. The Gay Games have opened up another avenue for individuals in the LGBT community to connect.

The Federation of Gay Games Records documents the activities of the federation and each Gay Games event. The bulk of the collection was donated to the Hormel Center in 1997 and several additions have been made since then. Although the materials from Gay Games I-III are relatively small, the materials for Gay Games IV are fairly complete. As this is an active organization, the library expects the Gay Games archives to grow in the years to come.

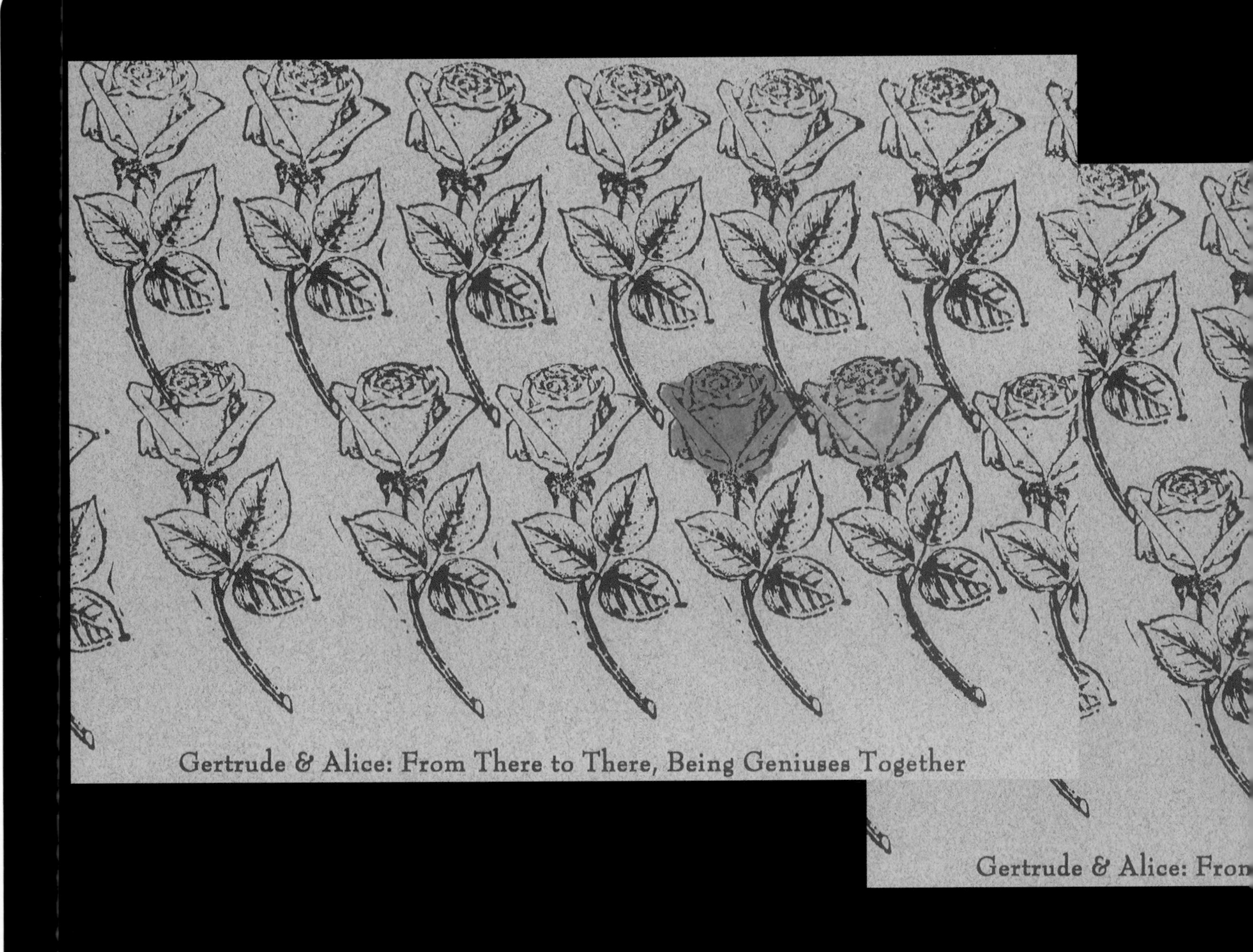

HORMEL CENTER PROGRAMS & EXHIBITIONS

1996–2005

Exhibitions and public programming are a crucial component of the James C. Hormel Gay and Lesbian Center. Whether curated by library staff, developed by community groups, or proposed by individuals, exhibitions make the center interactive on a daily basis. Similarly, the well-attended public programs offer an opportunity for experts to provide information and stimulate community discussion on a wide range of important topics. This list contains most of the major exhibitions and a selective sampling of the over one hundred programs the Hormel Center has hosted since opening in 1996. It provides an indication of the diversity of the center's offerings and partnerships and a window into some of the most salient issues within the LGBT community. Listed exhibitions took place in the Hormel Center unless otherwise noted.

1996

PROGRAMS

Parents, Families, and Friends of Lesbians and Gays (PFLAG) Talks Series:
– Evan Wolfson on gay marriage
– Abraham Verghese, author of *My Own Country*
– Jonathan Ned Katz, author of *The Invention of Homosexuality*
Cosponsored by the Bay Area Council of PFLAG

EXHIBITIONS

Into the Light: The Making of the Hormel Center Mural
Curated by Peter Christian Haberkorn, Barbara Levine, and Paige Ramey

Gay by the Bay: A History of Queer Culture in the San Francisco Bay Area
Curated by Susan Stryker and Jim Van Buskirk

Photographs by Cathy Cade and Joan Bobkoff of lesbian, gay, and bisexual youth for *Free Your Mind: The Book for Gay, Lesbian, and Bisexual Youth—and Their Allies*, by Ellen Bass and Kate Kaufman

Cracks in the Iron Closet: Travels in Gay and Lesbian Russia
Curated by David Tuller

Shedding a Straightjacket [sic]: Homophile Civil Rights/Homosexual Liberation, 1961-66, organized the GLBT Historical Society

Otras Cosas / Other Things: Mixed media sculpture by Sandra Ortiz Taylor

1997

PROGRAMS

PFLAG Talks Series:
– Kevin Jennings on "Making Schools Safe for Gay Youth"
– Simon LeVay on "Biology of Sexual Orientation"
– Mitzi Henderson, PFLAG President, 1992-1997, on "Straight Talk About Gay People"
Cosponsored by the Bay Area Council of PFLAG

Desire and Sexuality in Germany 1910–1945 Series:
– "Jewish Berlin, the Twenties and Sexology," with David Biale
– "Magnus Hirschfeld and Transgender Identity," with Susan Stryker

EXHIBITIONS

Tom Cline: Selected Works: AIDS-related sculpture

Sappho: No Ordinary Housewife!, curated by the Sappho Project

BUTCH / FTM

Building Coalitions Through Dialogue

Saturday, March 28

10:00 am - 4:00 pm

(Registration begins at 9:00 am)

Location: SF Main Library, 100 Larkin, Koret Auditorium; Civic Center

Free, donations gladly accepted

e goal of this day is to build coalitions through dialogue between butch lesbian/dyke communities and FTM/ trans mmunities. In a hostile social and political climate, we often find ourselves struggling with prejudice and oppression in lation from each other. The format will include panel discussions and smaller group settings.

All genders encouraged to attend and participate.

This is part of an on-going series of dialogues planned between communities of various sexual and gender identities.
This event is co-sponsored by The Harvey Milk Institute &
The James C. Hormel Gay & Lesbian Center of the San Francisco Public Library.

In addition to the panels, smaller group topics include:
How do Butches & FTM's identify differently, the same?
Community Building
Betrayal: What Makes It Hard to Trust Each Other?

BUTCH / FTM

Building Coalitions Through Dialogue

Saturday, March 28

10:00 am - 4:00 pm

(Registration begins at 9:00 am)

Location: SF Main Library, 100 Larkin, Koret Auditorium; Civic Center

Free, donations gladly accepted

The goal of this day is to build coalitions through dialogue between butch lesbian/dyke communities and FTM/ trans communities. In a hostile social and political climate, we often find ourselves struggling with prejudice and oppression in isolation from each other. The format will include panel discussions and smaller group settings.

All genders encouraged to attend and participate.

This is part of an on-going series of dialogues planned between communities of various sexual and gender identities.
This event is co-sponsored by The Harvey Milk Institute &
The James C. Hormel Gay & Lesbian Center of the San Francisco Public Library.

In addition to the panels, smaller group topics include:
How do Butches & FTM's identify differently, the same?
Community Building
Betrayal: What Makes It Hard to Trust Each Other?

For Registration & Information:

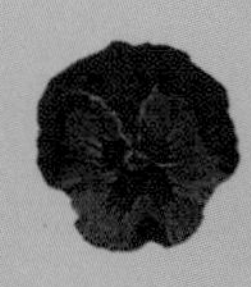

Harvey Milk Institute
584-B Castro Street #451
San Francisco, CA 94114
415/552-7200, E-mail: HarvMilk@aol.com

BUTCH / FTM

Building Coalitions Through Dialogue

Saturday, March 28

10:00 am - 4:00 pm

(Registration begins at 9:00 am)

cation: SF Main Library, 100 Larkin, Koret Auditorium; Civic Center

Free, donations gladly accepted

of this day is to build coalitions through dialogue between butch lesbian/dyke communities and FTM/ trans ties. In a hostile social and political climate, we often find ourselves struggling with prejudice and oppression in from each other. The format will include panel discussions and smaller group settings.

All genders encouraged to attend and participate.

part of an on-going series of dialogues planned between communities of various sexual and gender identities.
This event is co-sponsored by The Harvey Milk Institute &
The James C. Hormel Gay & Lesbian Center of the San Francisco Public Library.

In addition to the panels, smaller group topics include:
How do Butches & FTM's identify differently, the same?
Community Building
Betrayal: What Makes It Hard to Trust Each Other?

egistration & Information:

The Life and Times of Magnus Hirschfeld
Curated by Mel Gordon

Crimes Against Nature, 1977–1997, 20th anniversary of the Gay Men's Theatre Collective: performance piece

Founding a Dynasty: Jose Sarria, the Black Cat, and the San Francisco Imperial Court System, organized by the GLBT Historical Society

Particular Voices: Portraits of Gay & Lesbian Writers by Robert Giard (Skylight Gallery)

1998

PROGRAMS

Butch/FTM: Building Coalitions Through Dialogue
Panel discussions and small group meetings cosponsored by the Harvey Milk Institute

Lambda Literary Awards–Northern California Nominees Reading and Reception, cosponsored by the Lambda Literary Foundation

Remembering Harvey Milk: A Personal View
Slide lecture by Daniel Nicoletta

Kwanzaa Celebration: cosponsored by Lesbians and Gays of African Descent for Democratic Action and the African American Center at SFPL

EXHIBITIONS

T-shirt Exhibit: Selections from the Hormel Center's Collection Documenting LGBT History

Gertrude & Alice: From There to There Being Geniuses Together
Curated by Hans Gallas

Lesbian Family Portraits:
"Women in Love" photographs by Barbara Seyda and Diane Herrera and "Lesbian Mothering" photographs by Cathy Cade (Jewett Gallery)

Charles Molle: 50 Years by the Bay, curated by Ken Maley

Lesbian Crusaders: The Del Martin, Phyllis Lyon and Daughters of Bilitis Collection, organized by the GLBT Historical Society

Sylvester Metamorphosis: From Cockette to Disco Diva
Organized by the GLBT Historical Society

1999

PROGRAMS

Disability rights for people living with HIV/AIDS, mental illness, or other disabilities
Panel discussion on the Americans with Disabilities Act

Queer at the End of the Century series:
"Creating Our History," "Defending Our History," and "Surviving Our History"

EXHIBITIONS

oPINionated: A Sampling of Queer Lapel Pins & Buttons from the Hormel Center Collection

The White Night Riots Remembered: Commemorating the 20th Anniversary of the Demonstrations

Visible Injuries: Looking at Abuse and Violence in Same-Sex Relationships
Curated by Patrick Letellier

The Illusion of Conformity: Don Lucas and Sleight-of-Hand Activism in San Francisco, 1953–1969
Organized by the GLBT Historical Society

Mixed Media: Gay Images in the Straight Media, Straight Images in the Gay Media, 1938–1998

2000

PROGRAMS

TimesTalks: Breaking the Silence: Gays & Lesbians in Professional Sports
Panel discussion cosponsored by the *New York Times*

TimesTalks: Digital Diversity: The Growth of the Gay & Lesbian Online Marketplace
Panel discussion cosponsored by the *New York Times*

Harry Hay and the Founding of the Mattachine Society: A 50th Anniversary Celebration

EXHIBITIONS

Strange Sisters: The Art of Lesbian Pulp Fiction

Sheets in the Wind: A History of the Poster in the LGBT Community
Organized by the GLBT Historical Society

Making a Case for Community History: bisexual, youth, elderly, sex workers, Sisters of Perpetual Indulgence, Native Americans, and founders of the Women's Building
Organized by the GLBT Historical Society

Lost and Found: A Museum of Lesbian Memory:
Kim Anno and E. G. Crichton

2001

PROGRAMS

Broadway's Gay Tunesmiths: Lorenz Hart and Cole Porter, audio
Lecture by Bonnie Weiss

Intersexuality: Redefining Sex: A Dialog, video/panel discussion

Kirk Read reads from *How I Learned to Snap*

Omnigender: A Trans-Religious Approach
Lecture by Virginia Mollencott

EXHIBITIONS

Queer Folk Art, organized by the GLBT Historical Society

Looking Trans, curated by Jordy Jones for Trans-Art 2001

Megahood: The Origin & Evolution of the Folsom Street Fair
Organized by the GLBT Historical Society

POSITIVE: Art by artists living with AIDS
Curated by Visual AID (Skylight Gallery)

2002

PROGRAMS

High School Survival Strategies for Poets and Queers, author reading

Times Talks: "The Commercial Closet, GLBT Images in Advertising"
Rick Lyman and Michael Wilke

Alternated Channels: The Story of GLBT Television Images
Video lecture by Steven Capsuto

Celebrating the Life and Work of Steve Abbott, World AIDS Day event

EXHIBITIONS

We Love You Alice B. Toklas, curated by Hans Gallas

Butterflies and Oranges: 25th Anniversary of the 1977 Butterfly Brigade, organized by the GLBT Historical Society

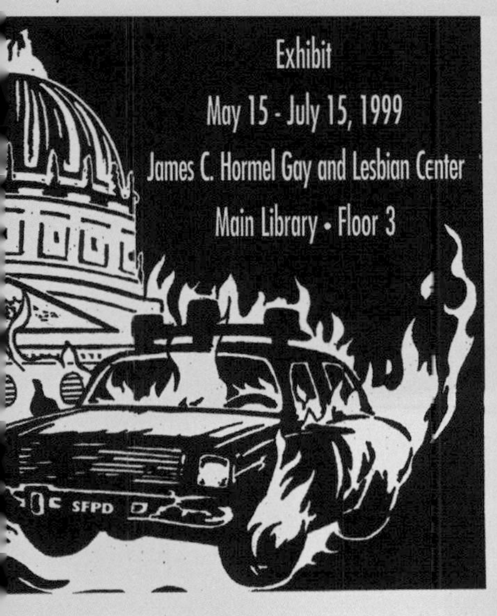

Opening the Closet Door: Photographs of the Early Gay Rights Movement by Kay Tobin Lahusen

Intergeneration: Creative Encounters, curated by Frank Pietronigro

Domestic Intelligence, book arts by Lisa Kokin

Robert Giard–In Memoriam

Discovering Passions, Evolving Bodies: GLBT Periodicals Since World War II, organized by the GLBT Historical Society

Gay Presses of New York, curated by Felice Picano

2003

PROGRAMS

Queer Bollywood: Alternative Sexualities in Popular Indian Cinema
Video lecture

Raymond Luczak: Deaf/Gay Poet/Filmmaker
Performance cosponsored by the Deaf Services Center at SFPL

A Date with Kate (in your face) Bornstein: Transgender Performance Artist, author interviewed by Carol Queen

Lavender and Green: Queer Irish Writing
Group author reading

Learning to be Old: Gender, Culture and Aging in the GLBT Community
Reading by Margaret Cruikshank

Queer & Jewish or Jewish & Queer? Writers Wrestling with Issues of Identity, panel discussion cosponsored by Congregation Sha'ar Zahav

Queer Crips: Disabled Gay Men and Their Stories
Readings, performance, and celebration

EXHIBITIONS

Loss Is a Blossom, mixed-media artwork by Gregg Cassin

Lost on Twilight Road: Uncovering the Golden Age of Gay Male Pulps, from the Hormel Center's Collection

Unfurling Pride: Gilbert Baker's Rainbow Flag Turns 25
Organized by the GLBT Historical Society

ueer Britannia

tion of Gay Men in British Film

Large Screen Videos

SCHEDULE FOR JUNE 2001

HURSDAYS AT NOON, KORET AUDITORIUM

San Francisco Public Library Presents

Queer Britannia

A Celebration of Gay Men in British Film

Large Screen Videos

SCHEDULE FOR JUNE 2001

THURSDAYS AT NOON, KORET AUDITORIUM

Thursdays at Noon
Koret Auditorium
Main Library, Lower Level
All programs at the Library are free.

June 7

Victim (1962, 100 min.) Dirk Bogarde starred in this groundbreaking thriller about an attorney who goes after a ring of blackmailers targeting gay men. Made when homosexuality was still a crime in England, this powerful film was a courageous undertaking for all involved.

June 14

Sunday Bloody Sunday (1971, 110 min.) Glenda Jackson and Peter Finch are both vying for the affections of the same young man (Murray Head) in this critically acclaimed John Schlesinger film.

June 21

The Naked Civil Servant (1975, 110 min.) John Hurt won the British Academy Award for his portrayal of colorful gay pioneer Quentin Crisp in this British television adaptation of Crisp's autobiography.

June 28

Prick Up Your Ears (1987, 111 min.) Stephen Frears' film biography of '60s playwright Joe Orton (Gary Oldman) provides a frank look at his private life, including public sex and his murder at the hands of lover Kenneth Halliwell (Alfred Molina). Vanessa Redgrave costars as Orton's agent Peggy Ramsay.

Cosponsored by the Audio Visual Center, the James C. Hormel Gay and Lesbian Center and supported by the Friends & Foundation of the San Francisco Public Library

San Francisco Public Library
100 Larkin Street @ Grove, 415-557-4277

June 7

Victim (1962, 100 min.) Dirk Bogarde starred in this groundbreaking thriller about an attorney who goes after a ring of blackmailers targeting gay men. Made when homosexuality was still a crime in England, this powerful film was a courageous undertaking for all involved.

Thursdays at Noon
Koret Auditorium
Main Library, Lower Level
All programs at the Library are free.

June 14

Sunday Bloody Sunday (1971, 110 min.) Glenda Jackson and Peter Finch are both vying for the affections of the same young man (Murray Head) in this critically acclaimed John Schlesinger film.

June 21

The Naked Civil Servant (1975, 110 min.) John Hurt won the British Academy Award for his portrayal of colorful gay pioneer Quentin Crisp in this British television adaptation of Crisp's autobiography.

June 28

Prick Up Your Ears (1987, 111 min.) Stephen Frears' film biography of '60s playwright Joe Orton (Gary Oldman) provides a frank look at his private life, including public sex and his murder at the hands of lover Kenneth Halliwell (Alfred Molina). Vanessa Redgrave costars as Orton's agent Peggy Ramsay.

Cosponsored by the Audio Visual Center, the James C. Hormel Gay and Lesbian Center and supported by the Friends & Foundation of the San Francisco Public Library

COCKTAILS: The Art of Kim Bach and Hilary Lorenz

November 1978: Harvey Milk, 1930–1978
Commemoration of the assassination of a political leader

2004

PROGRAMS

Radar Reading Series, author readings hosted by Michelle Tea

Queer Photo Salon
Photography slide show hosted by Chloe Atkins

Dangerous Families: Queer Writing on Surviving
Book launch party

The Vision and Voice of Two FTM Pioneers: Loren Cameron and Jamison Green, author/artist reading and celebration

At the Crossroads of Desire: a Celebration of African Diasporic Spirit in the LGBT Community, author reading and celebration

Mani's Story: Yellow is for Hermaphrodites
Documentary film screening and author interview

EXHIBITIONS

Reversing Vandalism: Destroyed Books Transformed into Art
(Hormel Center, Jewett Gallery, Grove Street exhibition cases)

The San Francisco Dyke March
Photographs by Jane Cleland and Cathy Cade

Mining the Archive: A Story of San Francisco's Leather Community from the Leather Archives and Museum in Chicago

Queer Movie Poster Show, curated by Jenni Olson

Rattlesnake in a Moving Car: Life with HIV
Art installation by Rob Anderson

The San Francisco Public Library Presents

LOOKING TRANS

TRANS ART 2001

EXHIBITION
May 4 - June 4, 2001

An exhibit of visual work that looks at a range of transgender experiences, subjectivities and personal gestures.

Exhibition
The Hormel Center
San Francisco Main Library
100 Larkin Street, Third Floor

Artists
- Del La Gra
- Cooper L
- Jordy Jon
- Chloe Atk
- Loren Ca

Opening Reception
Friday, May 4, 2001 • 6:00 to
GLBT Historical Society
973 Market Street, Suite 400

The exhibition continues at the Hormel
may be viewed during regular Library

Trans Art 2001 is co-sponsored by The
Historical Society of Northern California
San Francisco Public Library

All programs at t

San Francisc

Main Library 100 Larki

The San Francisco Public Library Presents

LOOKING TRANS

TRANS ART 2001

EXHIBITION

May 4 - June 4, 2001

An exhibit of visual work that looks at a range of transgender experiences, subjectivities and personal gestures.

Exhibition
The Hormel Center
San Francisco Main Library
100 Larkin Street, Third Floor

Artists

- Del La Grace Volcano • Erin O'Neill
- Cooper Lee Bombardier • Annie Sprinkle
- Jordy Jones • Hans Scheirl & Svar Simpson,
- Chloe Atkins • Kaspar Jivan Sexana,
- Loren Cameron • Saimon Li

Opening Reception
Friday, May 4, 2001 • 6:00 to 9:00 PM
GLBT Historical Society
973 Market Street, Suite 400

The exhibition continues at the Hormel Center and may be viewed during regular Library hours.

Trans Art 2001 is co-sponsored by The Gay, Lesbian, Bisexual, and Transgender Historical Society of Northern California and The James C. Hormel of The San Francisco Public Library

All programs at the Library are free.

San Francisco Public Library

Main Library 100 Larkin Street @ Grove 415.557.4277

2005

PROGRAMS

Queer Beats: How the Beats Turned America On to Sex
Regina Marler, author of *Queer Beats* and Thea Hillman, Kirk Read, Kevin Killian, Catherine French, and Joel Tan discuss the Beat generation and their continuing impact on literature today.

Gay Marriage: State of the Heart
Celebrating the first anniversary of the marriages performed at San Francisco City Hall. Screening of documentary, *One Wedding and a Revolution*, followed by panel discussion including: Betty Berzon, Kate Kendell, Mark Leno, Molly McKay, and Sylvia Rhue.

Valencia Rose Revisited: Early Queer Theater
To commemorate the twentieth anniversary of its closing in 1985, Tom Ammiano, Doug Holsclaw, Ron Lanza, Karen Ripley, and F. Allen Sawyer reminisce about one of the city's most prominent queer theatrical venues.

EXHIBITIONS

Icons: Etchings and Monotypes by Andrew Ogus

Nazi Persecution of Homosexuals 1933–1945
Organized by the United States Holocaust Memorial Museum
(Skylight Gallery)

Magnus Hirschfeld 1868–1935
Curated by Gerard Koskovich
(Skylight Gallery)

Out at the Library: Celebrating the James C. Hormel Gay and Lesbian Center
(Hormel Center, Jewett Gallery, Eureka Valley Branch)

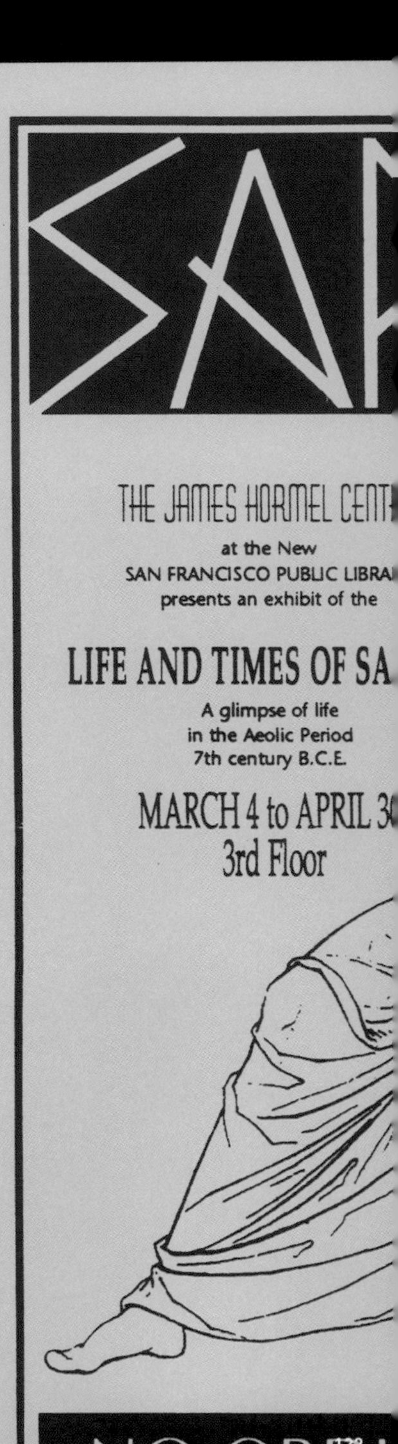

SAPPHO

THE JAMES HORMEL CENTER

at the New
SAN FRANCISCO PUBLIC LIBRARY
presents an exhibit of the

LIFE AND TIMES OF SAPPHO

A glimpse of lif
in the Aeolic Peri
7th century B.C.

MARCH 4 to API
3rd Floor

Y HOUSEWIFE

THE JAMES HORMEL CENTER

at the New
SAN FRANCISCO PUBLIC LIBRARY
presents an exhibit of the

LIFE AND TIMES OF SAPPHO

A glimpse of life
in the Aeolic Period
7th century B.C.E.

MARCH 4 to APRIL 30
3rd Floor

NO ORDINARY HOUSEWIFE

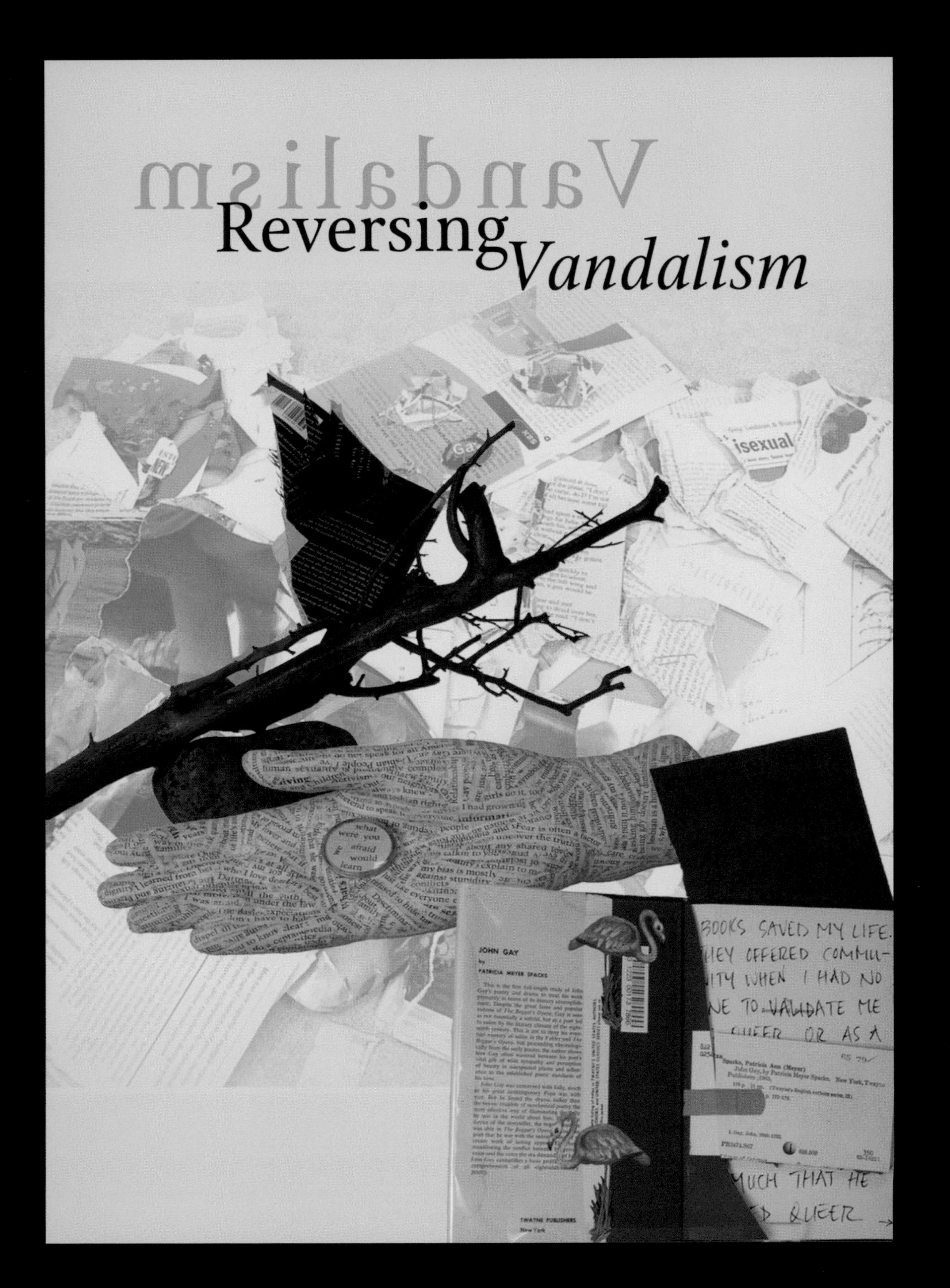

Barbara McMahan
Reversing Vandalism announcement
2004

RIGHT:
Reversing Vandalism
Jewett Gallery, San Francisco
Main Library

Reversing Vandalism

Destroyed Books Transformed into Art

January 31–May 2, 2004

Presented by the Hormel Center, the *Reversing Vandalism* exhibition was on view in three venues at the Main Library from January 31–May 2, 2004. Filling the Jewett Gallery, the Hormel Center itself, and inaugurating the new Grove Street exhibition case, this was the largest art exhibition undertaken to date by the San Francisco Public Library. Seen by nearly 12,000 visitors, the exhibition generated a buzz equal to the original call for participation and resulted in extensive media coverage and several related projects. In conjunction with the exhibition, the Hormel Center sponsored community panels including "How Communities Can Transform Hate into Healing" and "The Art of Altered Books." An online version of the exhibition was developed, and in the fall of 2004, the Friends of the San Francisco Public Library held a silent auction of works donated by artists with proceeds benefiting library services. The story continues to be told; *Reversing Vandalism* is one of five stories featured in *Not In Our Town Northern California: When Hate Happens Here*, a documentary produced by The Working Group that examines the negative effects of intolerance and profiles creative and effective tools communities have developed to fight hate.

Reversing Vandalism

In early 2001, San Francisco Public Library staff began finding books hidden under shelving units throughout the main library. The books had been carved with a sharp instrument: covers and inner pages were slashed and odd almond-shaped pieces were cut out. As the mutilated books began accumulating, staff recognized that most of the volumes were related to issues of gay, lesbian, bisexual, and transgendered individuals, HIV/AIDS, and women's health issues. Staff members worked together to help find and inventory the over 600 damaged books, as well as to observe the stacks waiting for someone to shove damaged books under a shelf.

Eventually the vandal was caught by a librarian, on her day off, who alerted library security. The perpetrator was arrested and charged with a hate crime. When the reports of the crime hit the newspapers, an outpouring of support as well as offers to help replace the volumes came from sympathizers across the country. After the damaged books were returned by the San Francisco Police Department, most of them were determined to be beyond repair and would be withdrawn from the collection. As the volumes were digitally documented, it was felt that discarding the books would only complete the vandal's crime.

In conversation with local visual artists, library staff from the Hormel Center and the Office of Exhibitions and Programming developed the process leading to the *Reversing Vandalism* project. A public call for participation was circulated offering the destroyed books to artists, community members, and interested individuals. Response to the project was immediate and intense as word rapidly spread beyond the Bay Area. The library received book requests from nearly 1,000 amateur and professional artists from around the world. People quickly understood that this vandalism was not solely about gay and lesbian issues or even about books, but represented a social climate increasingly filled with fear and hate.

Ultimately over 200 participants from more than twenty states as well as Japan and France contributed work in a wide range of media: works on paper, sculptures, assemblages, textiles, paintings, photography, even a working clock. The range of responses was as varied as the artists themselves. Some of these artists' responses were whimsical, sad, angry, political, and each had a story to tell. Artist statements were exhibited alongside their artwork. Many created something beautiful from the shreds of a ruined book. Others added humor to the situation. Most impressive was the wide variety of artwork. Using basically the same raw materials, artists contributed an unexpectedly diverse range of expression as they participated in proselytizing the importance of reversing vandalism.

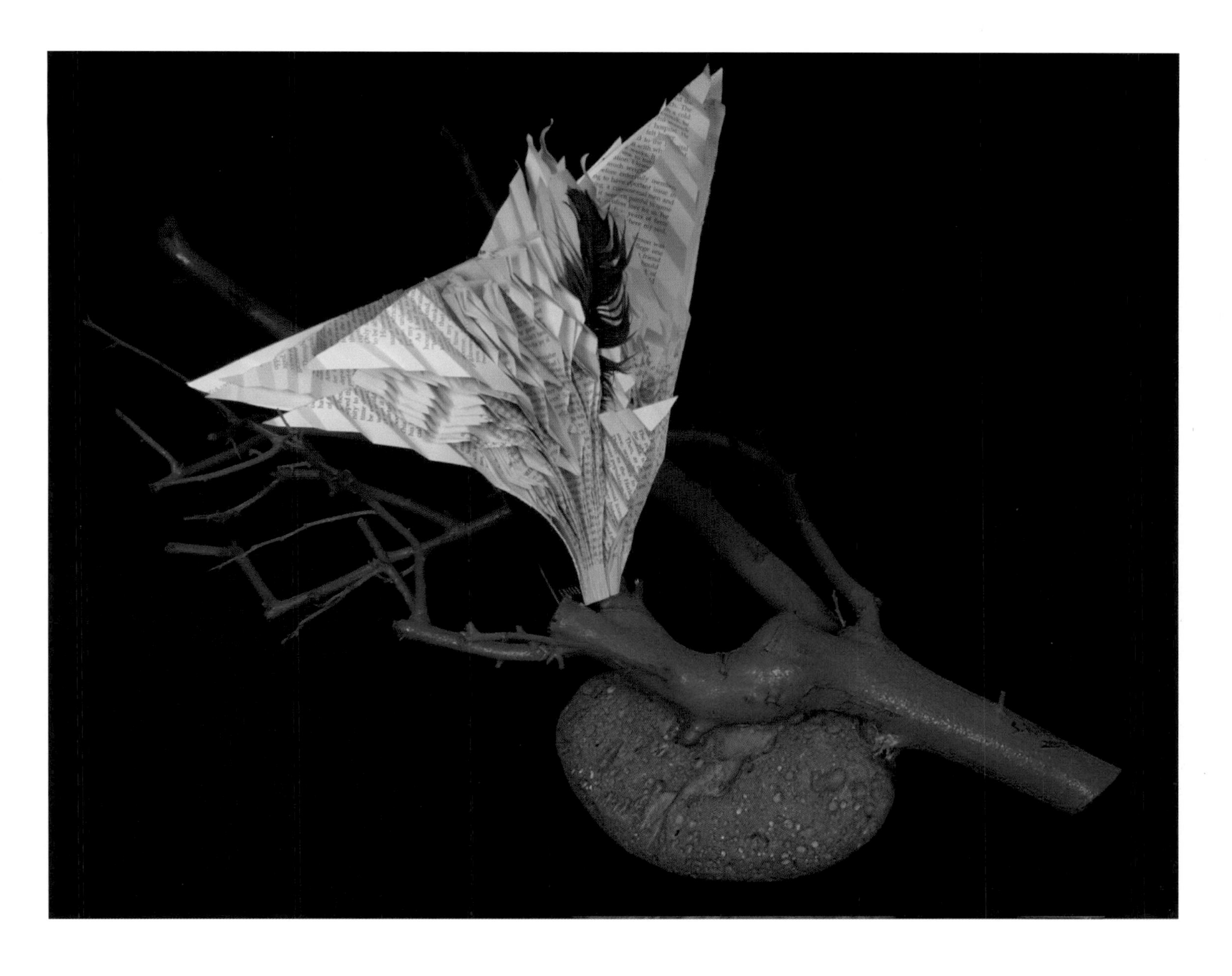

Sherry Karver

Blackbird Singing, 2003

Mixed media

Private Collection

Vandalized book: *Fighting Words, Personal Essays by Black Gay Men*

Edited by Charles Michael Smith, Avon Books, 1999

Artist statement: I had decided before receiving the book that I would let whatever shape the book was in dictate the direction that the art should go. The way in which the book had been vandalized made it look somewhat like a bird, so that became the theme. The bird is symbolic of regeneration, like the Phoenix rising from the ashes. It was important to create a bird/book that exemplified rebirth, hope, freedom, and soaring to greater heights. The blue branch represents the sky, giving peace and calmness and a safe haven for the bird. It is also to remind us to keep elevated thoughts. The branch is grounded in a rock to give it a strong foundation on which to rest.

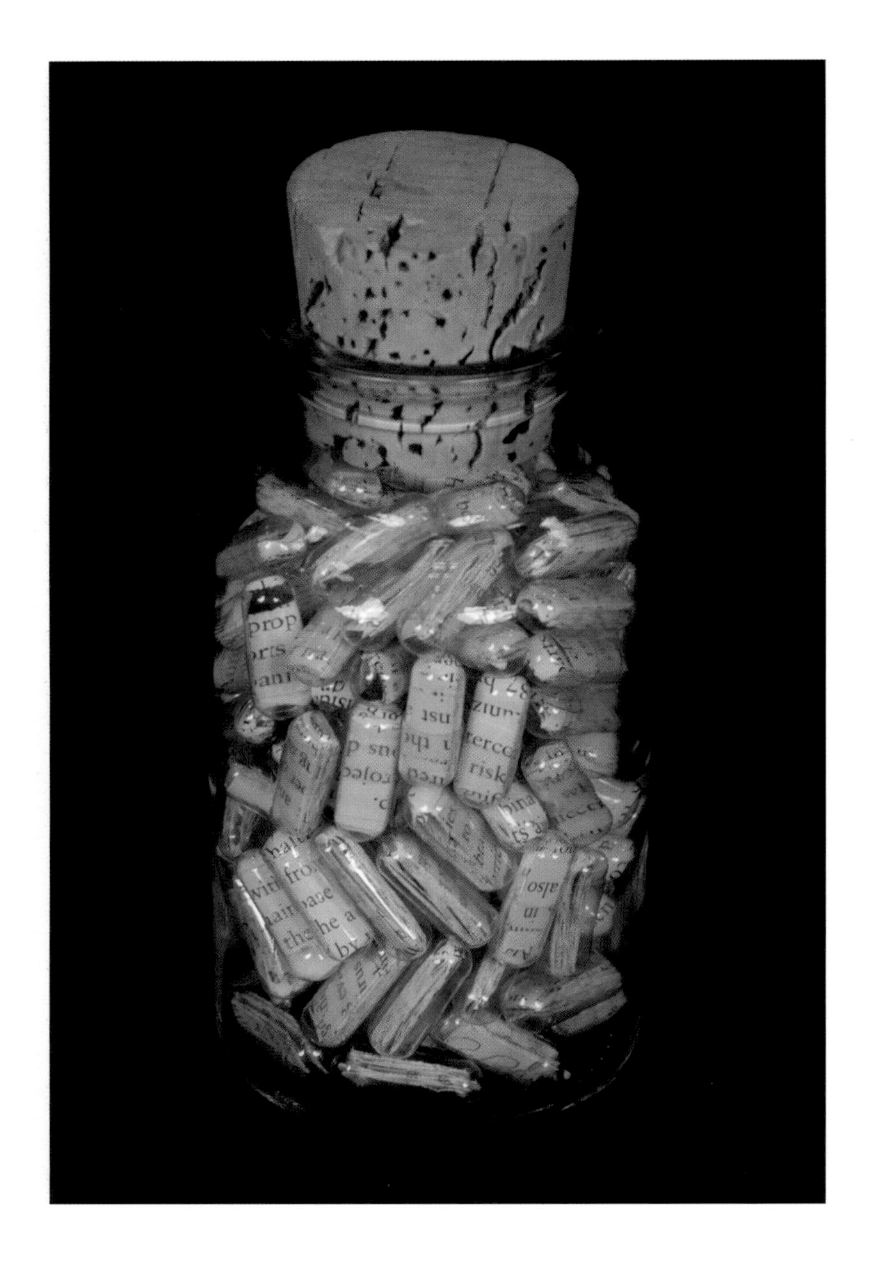

Cedar Marie

Best Medicine, 2003

Mixed media

Collection of Richard Meyer and David Román

Vandalized book: *AIDS & HIV in Perspective: A Guide to Understanding the Virus and its Consequences* by Barry D. Schoub, Cambridge University Press, 1994

Artist statement: *Best Medicine* evolved out of consideration for both the nature of the exhibition, *Reversing Vandalism*, and the title of the vandalized book, *AIDS & HIV in Perspective, A Guide to Understanding the Virus and its Consequences*, by Barry D. Schoub. A vandal cut part of the book cover off and slashed its pages. This artwork addresses the issue of vandalism, expressed in the further destruction of the book by shredding the remaining contents. Enclosing the shreds in gel capsules, which could represent vitamins or medicine, creates an impossible paradox that could apply both to AIDS, which has no known cure, and to the book itself, which cannot be repaired.

F. Allen Sawyer

Untitled, 2003

Mixed media

Private Collection

Vandalized book: *Two Teenagers in Twenty: Writings by Gay and Lesbian Youth*, edited by Ann Heron, Alyson Publications, 1994

Percy Wise

TransPoetic #5, 2003

Mixed media

Collection of Mark Dresser

Vandalized book: *Trans Liberation: Beyond Pink or Blue*

by Leslie Feinberg, Beacon Press, 1998

Artist statement: It was at a staff meeting that the library security director held up copies of queer and feminist books that had been maliciously slashed. I couldn't help but cry. As a transgender artist and employee of the library, it was not an abstract of "the queer author" but close friends and family's words, pictures, and names I saw destroyed. One book was dedicated to an old friend—his name was slashed in half. This is the fifth piece in a series of artworks I call "TransPoetic." I admire and seek to elucidate the ways that poetry can cut discursively across historical events and identities. In each artwork, I seek to reposition transgender identities and meanings through words of past queer poets. Unfastened and flowing, poetic words seem to find poignant new authorship with an altered reading, swipe of a blade, or a refashioning mend of needle and thread. My first act of reclamation was simply to read this book. I chose not to alter it other than by obvious mending—it is still quite readable.

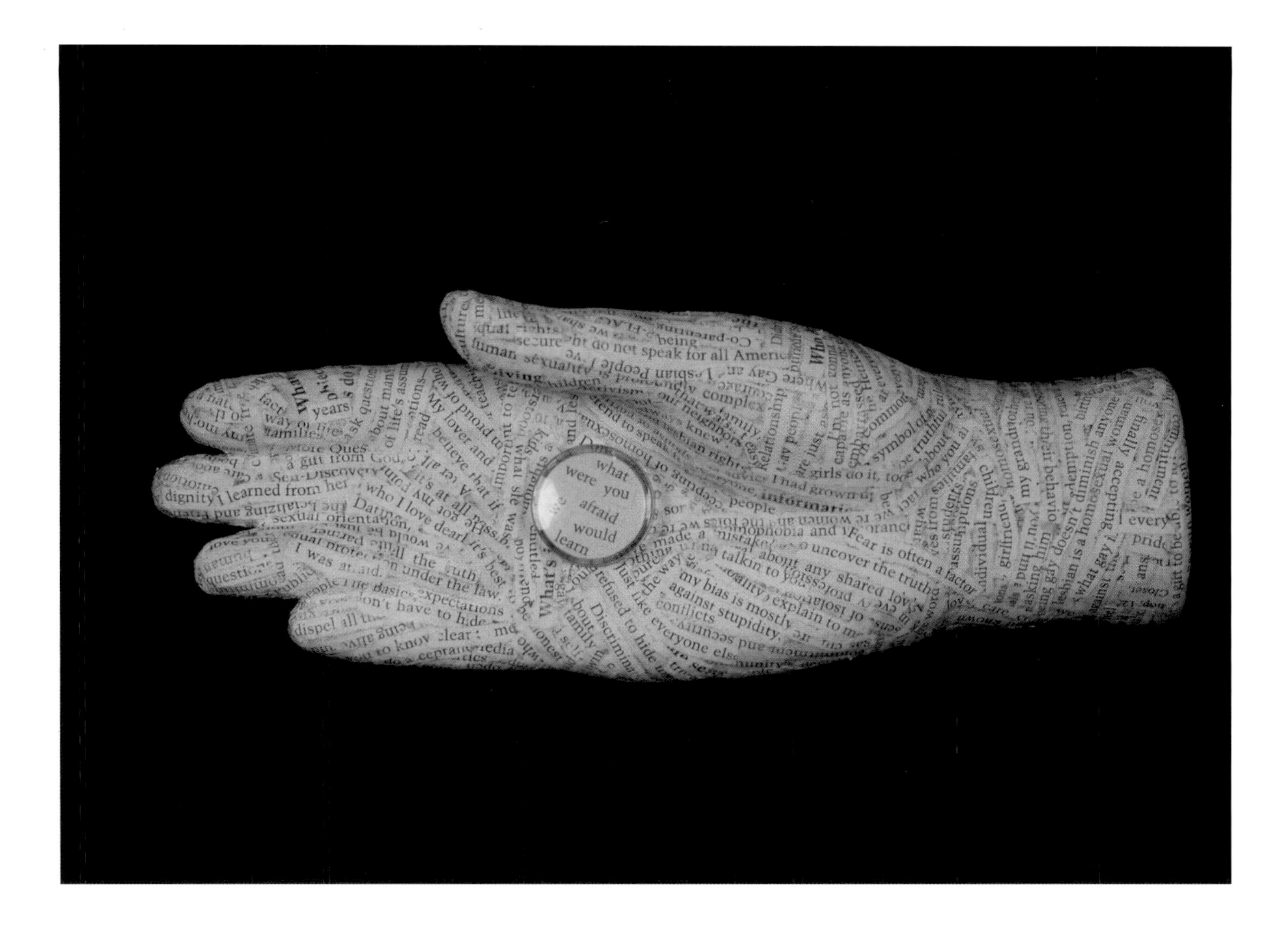

Dacey Hunter

For Duf, 2003

Mixed media

Private Collection

Vandalized book: *Is it a Choice?: answers to 300 of the most frequently asked questions about gays and lesbians* by Eric Marcus, Harper San Francisco, 1993

Artist statement: The inspiration for this sculpture came while reading (what was left of) *Is it a Choice?* Love, forgiveness, acceptance, understanding ... all of these are recurring themes in author Eric Marcus's "common sensitive" approach to exploring and explaining homosexuality ... and all are communicated in the simple gesture of an upturned palm. Papier-mâché and collage allowed me to connect with the text in an intimate way, and the deliberately primitive texture contrasts with the focal point of the work. The question posed is directed not only toward the Hormel Center's vandal, but to all who believe in censorship of the written word. The title of the piece is taken from the author's dedication to a friend "... who was never afraid to ask."

Carol Queen

Queering John Gay, 2003

(view of front and back covers)

Mixed media

Collection of Catherine King

Vandalized book: *John Gay* by Patricia Meyer Spacks,

Twayne Publishers, 1965

Artist statement: I received not a queer book but one that set off the vandal simply by its title. I worked to queerify a not-very-queer text and also to visualize, acknowledge, and partially heal the hate-induced damage to the book itself.

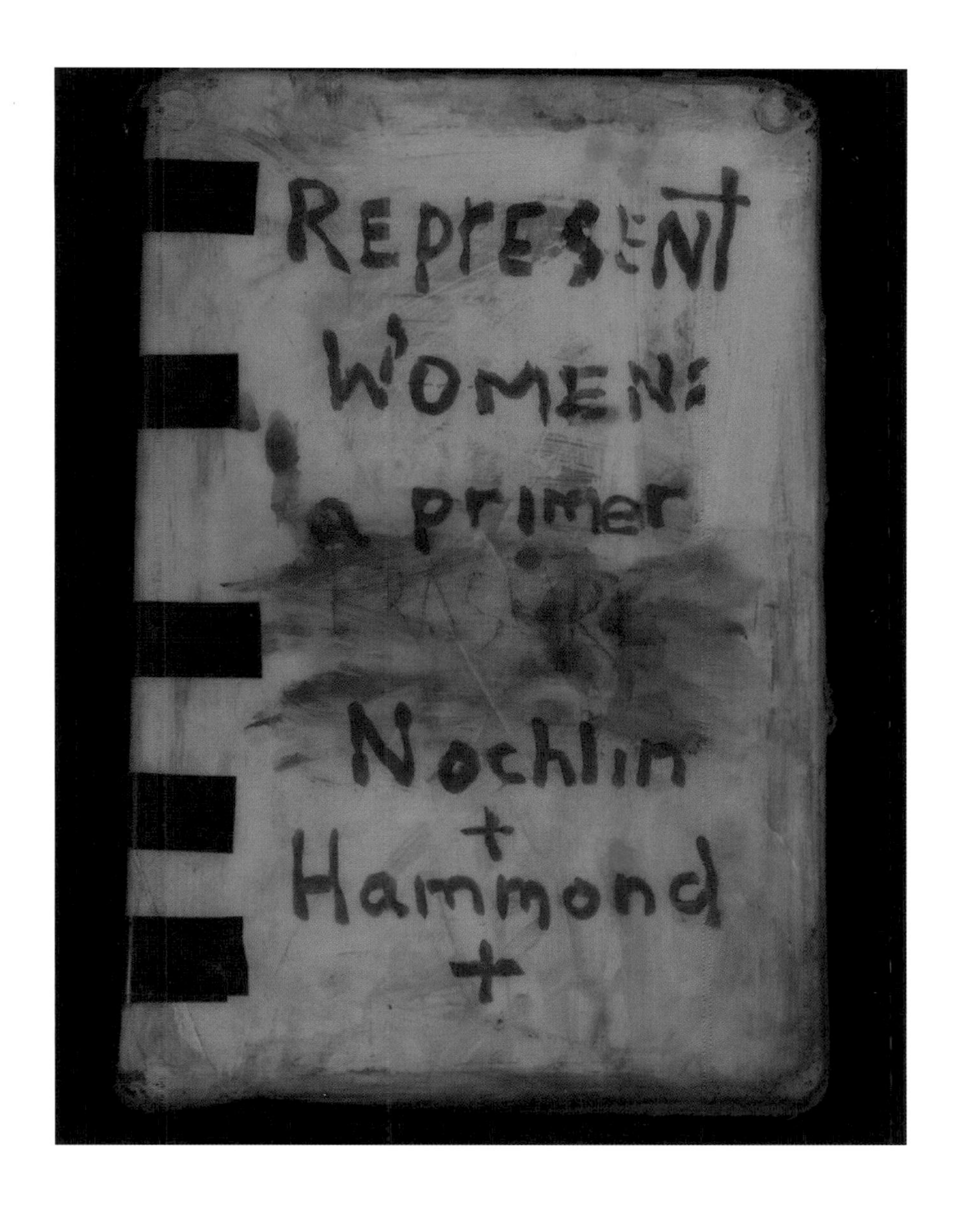

Harmony Hammond

Represent Women: A Primer, 2003

Mixed media

Collection of Richard Meyer and David Román

Vandalized book: *Representing Women* by Linda Nochlin, Thames & Hudson, 1999

Artist statement: I had read a lot of feminist art historian Linda Nochlin's insightful writing, but had not read this particular book examining how women were represented in the work of Gericault, Courbet, Degas, Seurat, and Cassatt, four men and one woman, as well as a chapter on the myth of the woman warrior and a chapter on the image of working women. The back half of the book was missing—sliced off at the spine after page 160. This was the chapter entitled "A House is Not a Home: Degas and the Subversion of the Family." It felt so violent to me. I knew that the art project allowed me to take the book apart and reconfigure it any way I wished. I could go large up to six feet square. Normally I work large, but here I found I wanted to keep the book format, to reconstitute the book whole, to (re)present women and women's bodies whole again. I made a new cover out of flesh-like latex rubber pages stained with red ochre/blood. The word "erasure," cut into the front cover functions as writing on the body and therefore bodies, referencing the intentionality of the vandalism.

Donating to the Hormel Center Archives

Archives view

The San Francisco Public Library's James C. Hormel Gay and Lesbian Center encourages donations of materials that might otherwise be lost to future generations. After reviewing the possible donation, library staff may accept the gift, or suggest other repositories that may be more appropriate.

Among the types of materials of interest to researchers in personal and family papers are

- Letters
- Diaries
- Scrapbooks
- Genealogical information
- Legal documents
- Memoirs/reminiscences
- Brochures, fliers and other ephemera
- Photographs/photo albums
- Films/videos/audiotapes
- Speeches/lectures
- Business records
- Subject files
- Drafts of published and unpublished writings

In addition, organizational records may include:

- Reports/minutes
- Correspondence
- Speeches
- Master copies of fliers, brochures, newspapers, and publications
- Artifacts

PREPARING YOUR COLLECTION FOR DONATION

Whenever possible, the library asks for your assistance in storing and preparing the materials for donation:

- Store collections in a cool, dry, dark place. Dampness, heat, and overexposure to dust and light promote decay.
- Moldy materials should be kept separately from other materials.
- Use acid-free storage materials (boxes, file folders, etc.) if possible.
- Identify the people whose letters are included.
- Label photographs, clippings, fliers, and memorabilia on the back with names, dates, and locations using a soft (#1 or #2) pencil.
- Avoid sticky photo albums; adhesive will ruin photos over time.
- Remove rubber bands and metal paper clips and staples, which deteriorate and damage paper over time. Use plastic paper clips if necessary.
- Unfold all papers so that they lie flat; creases tear more easily as paper ages.

- If duplicates exist, include only the best three copies.
- Print hard copies (i.e. paper copies) of all files on computer disks, in lieu of donating the disks. Hard copies mitigate the library's need to maintain a vast collection of software and hardware.

Please provide a biographical sketch and/or timeline of the major events in the individual's or organization's life to assist in arranging and describing the materials.

Donors will be asked to sign a donation agreement that states that the donor is transferring physical ownership and/or copyright to the library. Ownership of copyright is separate from ownership of the physical item. Assignment of copyright is often complex and library staff are available to consult with donors about the Deed of Gift.

Because library staff are not permitted to appraise the monetary value of a collection or to give tax advice, donors are encouraged to speak with their tax accountants or attorneys about the possibility of taking a tax deduction for the donation of a manuscript or archival collection to the library. The library can provide a list of qualified appraisers.

The library recognizes that sensitive material or private information may exist in individual or family papers, and is available to discuss options about specific donor concerns.

It is generally recommended that materials created by one person be kept together to facilitate research.

Once the materials are donated, the library will begin to prepare them so that they can be made available for researchers and the general public. In this way the past is preserved.

For more information, please contact:
The James C. Hormel Gay and Lesbian Center
San Francisco Public Library
100 Larkin Street
San Francisco, CA 94102
Phone: 415.557.4499
info@sfpl.org

The Hormel Endowment Committee

MEMBERS 1996–2005

Alvin H. Baum, Jr.

Charles Fernandez

Charles Q. Forester

Katherine V. Forrest

Adan Griego

Barbara Gittings

Jewelle L. Gomez

Roma P. Guy

Ambassador James C. Hormel (ex-officio)

Jeff Lewy

John Manzon-Santos

Zoon Nguyen

Felicia Park-Rogers

Joseph A. Rosenthal

Sherilyn Thomas

Timothy C. Wu

Vance M. Yoshida

Helen Zia

The Hormel Endowment Committee is a committee of the Friends of the San Francisco Public Library

Reproduction and Copyright Information

The San Francisco Public Library gratefully acknowledges the authors, photographers, artists, agents and publishers for their permission to use copyrighted material in *Out at the Library*. Every reasonable effort has been made to obtain all necessary permissions. Should any errors have occurred, they are inadvertent, and every effort will be made to correct them in subsequent editions, provided timely notification is made to the library in writing.

Unless otherwise noted, all materials in this book are drawn from the Hormel Center collections. Other library collections represented include:

The Daniel E. Koshland San Francisco History Center

The Marjorie G. & Carl W. Stern Book Arts & Special Collections Center:
- Robert Grabhorn Collection on the History of Printing & the Development of the Book
- James D. Phelan California Authors Collection
- Schmulowitz Collection of Wit & Humor

INFORMATION ORGANIZED BY BOOK SECTION AND PAGE NUMBER

FRONT MATTER AND INTRODUCTION

Cover image: Dr. Mary Walker's boots: Photograph by Dana Davis, 2005

Title page: Dr. Mary Walker's boots: Photograph by Dana Davis, 2005

Colophon/Table of Contents: Hormel Center Archives: Photograph by Dana Davis, 2005

4 Hormel Center: Photograph by Dana Davis, 2005

5 Reproduced courtesy of Douglas Menuez

6 Hormel Center: Photograph by Dana Davis, 2005

JUDY GRAHN: TRACKING PAST AND PRESENT

11 Reproduced courtesy of Lynda Koolish

16 Hormel Center: Photograph by Dana Davis, 2005

BARBARA LEVINE: FROM THE BEGINNING

19 Reproduced courtesy of Daniel Nicoletta

20 Hormel Center Archives: Photograph by Dana Davis, 2005

23 Reproduced courtesy of Daniel Nicoletta

24 Herb Caen Magazines and Newspapers Center (SFPL): Photograph by Dana Davis, 2005

27 Reproduced courtesy of Lynda Koolish

30 Reproduced courtesy of Chloe Atkins

THE HORMEL CENTER MURAL

35 Hormel Center mural: Photograph by Dana Davis, 2005

37 Hormel Center mural: Photograph by Dana Davis, 2005

JIM VAN BUSKIRK: REFLECTIONS

39 Reproduced courtesy of the Estate of Robert Giard

44 Reproduced courtesy of Rick Gerharter

EXPLORING THE ARCHIVES

45 Hormel Center Archives: Photograph by Dana Davis, 2005

46 Boxes containing Dr. Mary Walker's boots: Photograph by Dana Davis, 2005

48 Reproduced courtesy of Daniel Nicoletta

49 Dr. Mary Walker's boots, detail: Photograph by Dana Davis, 2005

51 Dr. Mary Walker's boots: Photograph by Dana Davis, 2005
Postcard reproduced courtesy of Helaine Victoria Press, Inc.

52 Reproduced courtesy of Stanford G. Gann Jr., of Levin and Gann, PA—Literary Executor of the Estate of Gertrude Stein

54 Postcard reproduced courtesy of Helaine Victoria Press, Inc.

55 *Two Poems*, reproduced courtesy of Stanford G. Gann Jr., of Levin and Gann, PA—Literary Executor of the Estate of Gertrude Stein. Book reproduced courtesy of the Robert Grabhorn Collection on the History of Printing & the Development of the Book, The Marjorie G. & Carl W. Stern Book Arts & Special Collections Center (SFPL)
A Book Concluding With As a Wife has a Cow, reproduced courtesy of Stanford G. Gann Jr., of Levin and Gann, PA—Literary Execu-

tor of the Estate of Gertrude Stein. Book reproduced courtesy of the Schmulowitz Collection of Wit & Humor, The Marjorie G. & Carl W. Stern Book Arts & Special Collections Center [SFPL]

57 Reproduced courtesy of Barbara Gittings

58 Reproduced courtesy of JEB [Joan E. Biren]

59 Elsa Gidlow correspondence reproduced courtesy of Celeste West of Booklegger Publishing and Marcelina Martin, www.marcelinamartin.com, co-executors of the Elsa Gidlow Estate. Letter reproduced courtesy of the GLBT Historical Society

Elsa Gidlow photograph reproduced courtesy of Lynda Koolish

61 Pulp paperback collection from Hormel Center Archives: Photograph by Dana Davis, 2005

68 Reproduced courtesy of the Estate of Robert Giard

70 *Barbara Grier*, reproduced courtesy of Lynda Koolish

Blackberri, reproduced courtesy of the Estate of Robert Giard

71 *Chrystos*, reproduced courtesy of Lynda Koolish

James Broughton, reproduced courtesy of the Estate of Robert Giard

72 *Pomo Afro Homos*, reproduced courtesy of the Estate of Robert Giard

Robert Duncan, reproduced courtesy of Lynda Koolish

73 Reproduced courtesy of Lynda Koolish

74 Reproduced courtesy of Robin Blaser, literary executor for the Estate of Jack Spicer; and the Jess Collins Trust. Book reproduced courtesy of the Robert Grabhorn Collection on the History of Printing & the Development of the Book, The Marjorie G. & Carl W. Stern Book Arts & Special Collections Center [SFPL]

75 Reproduced courtesy of Michelle Dunn and Annalee Dunn; and the Jess Collins Trust. Book reproduced courtesy of the Robert Grabhorn Collection on the History of Printing & the Development of the Book The Marjorie G. & Carl W. Stern Book Arts & Special Collections Center [SFPL]

76 Reproduced courtesy of the Literary Estate of Robert Duncan. Book reproduced courtesy of the James D. Phelan California Authors Collection, The Marjorie G. & Carl W. Stern Book Arts & Special Collections Center [SFPL]

77 *An Ode and Arcadia*, reproduced courtesy of the Literary Estate of Robert Duncan; and Robin Blaser, literary executor for the Estate of Jack Spicer. Book reproduced courtesy of the Robert Grabhorn Collection on the History of Printing & the Development of the Book, The Marjorie G. & Carl W. Stern Book Arts & Special Collections Center [SFPL]

Wichita Vortex Sutra, reproduced courtesy of Housmans Bookshop Ltd. and the Allen Ginsberg Trust, www.allenginsberg.org. Book reproduced courtesy of the James D. Phelan California Authors Collection, The Marjorie G. & Carl W. Stern Book Arts & Special Collections Center [SFPL]

78 Photograph reproduced courtesy of Fayette Hauser

80 *Offical Cockettes Paper Doll Book* reproduced courtesy of Ron Turner, Publisher, Last Gasp Press

82 *Gone Dollywood*, reproduced courtesy of David E. Johnston

Pinnocchio the Big Fag, reproduced courtesy of Keith Mayerson

83 *Fork Split*, reproduced courtesy of Jim Winters

Fresh Produce, reproduced courtesy of the Kiki Gallery Archive, administered by Wayne Smith; *Joan Jett-Blakk and Babette*, reproduced courtesy of the Kiki Gallery Archive, administered by Wayne Smith

Sick Joke, reproduced courtesy of Wayne Smith

84 Reproduced courtesy of the Estate of William Moritz

85 Reproduced courtesy of the Harry Hay Estate

86 Mattachine Society image reproduced courtesy of John Gruber

92-93 Reproduced courtesy of ONE National Gay & Lesbian Archives

95 Reproduced courtesy of Cathy Cade

97 Reproduced courtesy of Daniel E. Koshland San Francisco History Center [SFPL]

98 El Dorado Medallions: Photograph by Dana Davis, 2005

99 Reproduced courtesy of ACT UP San Francisco

100-101 William Billings scrapbook: Photograph by Dana Davis, 2005

104 Reproduced courtesy of Daniel Nicoletta

105 Photograph by Dana Davis, 2005

106 White Night Riot photograph reproduced courtesy of Daniel Nicoletta

White Night Riot front page reproduced courtesy of *The San Francisco Examiner*

107 Reproduced courtesy of Daniel Nicoletta

108 Reproduced courtesy of the Estate of Gary Fisher

110 Journals reproduced courtesy of Jewelle Gomez, photograph by Dana Davis, 2005

Vincent Diaries reproduced courtesy of Elizabeth Stone, photograph by Dana Davis, 2005

111 Reproduced courtesy of Ann P. Meredith

112 Gay Games posters reproduced courtesy of Federation of Gay Games: Photograph by Dana Davis, 2005

Gay Games medals reproduced courtesy of Federation of Gay Games: Photograph by Dana Davis, 2005

113 Reproduced courtesy of Federation of Gay Games: Photograph by Dana Davis, 2005

REVERSING VANDALISM

125 *Reversing Vandalism* installation at San Francisco Public Library: Photograph by Philip Cohen, 2004

127 Reproduced courtesy of Sherry Karver: Photograph by David Schwabe and Eric Monteiro, 2004

128 Reproduced courtesy of Cedar Marie: Photograph by David Schwabe and Eric Monteiro, 2004

129 Reproduced courtesy of F. Allen Sawyer: Photograph by David Schwabe and Eric Monteiro, 2004

130 Reproduced courtesy of Percy Wise: Photograph by David Schwabe and Eric Monteiro, 2004

131 Reproduced courtesy of Dacey Hunter: Photograph by David Schwabe and Eric Monteiro, 2004

132 Reproduced courtesy of Carol Queen: Photograph by David Schwabe and Eric Monteiro, 2004

133 Reproduced courtesy of Harmony Hammond: Photograph by David Schwabe and Eric Monteiro, 2004

DONATING TO THE HORMEL CENTER ARCHIVES

134 Hormel Center Archives: Photograph by Dana Davis, 2005

LAST PAGE

144 Reproduced courtesy of *San Francisco Chronicle*

Photographs by: Lacy Atkins, Paul Chinn, Deanne Fitzmaurice, Frederic Larson, Liz Mangelsdorf, and Lea Suzuki

Index

Bold numbers indicate pages containing imagery

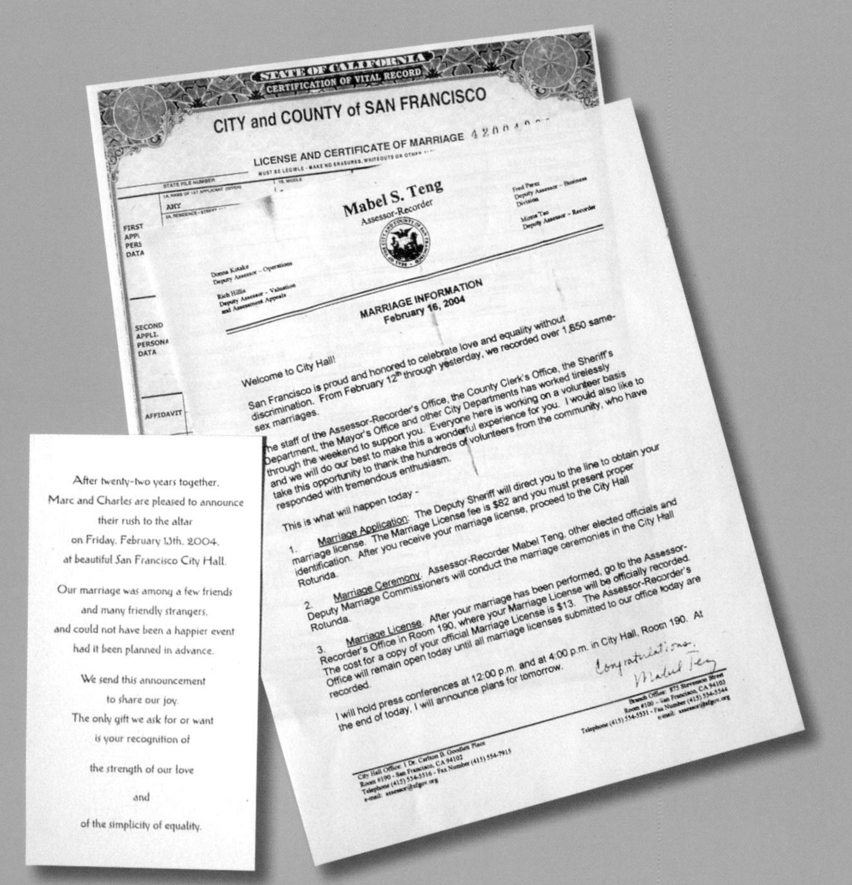

STATE OF CALIFORNIA
CERTIFICATION OF VITAL RECORD
CITY and COUNTY of SAN FRANCISCO
LICENSE AND CERTIFICATE OF MARRIAGE

Mabel S. Teng
Assessor-Recorder

Donna Kotake, Deputy Assessor – Operations
Rich Hillis, Deputy Assessor – Valuation and Assessment Appeals
Fred Perez, Deputy Assessor – Business Division
Minnie Tao, Deputy Assessor – Recorder

MARRIAGE INFORMATION
February 16, 2004

Welcome to City Hall!

San Francisco is proud and honored to celebrate love and equality without discrimination. From February 12th through yesterday, we recorded over 1,650 same-sex marriages.

The staff of the Assessor-Recorder's Office, the County Clerk's Office, the Sheriff's Department, the Mayor's Office and other City Departments has worked tirelessly through the weekend to support you. Everyone here is working on a volunteer basis and we will do our best to make this a wonderful experience for you. I would also like to take this opportunity to thank the hundreds of volunteers from the community, who have responded with tremendous enthusiasm.

This is what will happen today -

1. Marriage Application: The Deputy Sheriff will direct you to the line to obtain your marriage license. The Marriage License fee is $82 and you must present proper identification. After you receive your marriage license, proceed to the City Hall Rotunda.

2. Marriage Ceremony. Assessor-Recorder Mabel Teng, other elected officials and Deputy Marriage Commissioners will conduct the marriage ceremonies in the City Hall Rotunda.

3. Marriage License. After your marriage has been performed, go to the Assessor-Recorder's Office in Room 190, where your Marriage License will be officially recorded. The cost for a copy of your official Marriage License is $13. The Assessor-Recorder's Office will remain open today until all marriage licenses submitted to our office today are recorded.

I will hold press conferences at 12:00 p.m. and at 4:00 p.m. in City Hall, Room 190. At the end of today, I will announce plans for tomorrow.

Congratulations,
Mabel Teng

City Hall Office: 1 Dr. Carlton B. Goodlett Place, Room #190 - San Francisco, CA 94102, Telephone (415) 554-5516 - Fax Number (415) 554-7915, e-mail: assessor@sfgov.org

Branch Office: 875 Stevenson Street, Room #100 - San Francisco, CA 94103, Telephone (415) 554-5531 - Fax Number (415) 554-5544, e-mail: assessor@sfgov.org

After twenty-two years together,
Marc and Charles are pleased to announce
their rush to the altar
on Friday, February 13th, 2004,
at beautiful San Francisco City Hall.

Our marriage was among a few friends
and many friendly strangers,
and could not have been a happier event
had it been planned in advance.

We send this announcement
to share our joy.
The only gift we ask for or want
is your recognition of
the strength of our love
and
of the simplicity of equality.

TOP TO BOTTOM:
Gay marriage clippings from the San Francisco Chronicle
February 13–24, 2004

Gay marriage materials, **2004**

ALL MATERIALS:
SAN FRANCISO HISTORY CENTER